RUMOURS OF SPRING

Praise for *Rumours of Spring*

'A terrifying yet tender account of a girlhood spent under near-constant siege. Farah Bashir's story is especially instructive to those of us who cannot conceive of the insidious, often invisible, harm that thirty years of violence has wrought upon so many families in Kashmir. I found *Rumours of Spring* to be beautiful, painful and utterly revelatory.'

— MADHURI VIJAY, author of *The Far Field*

'Extraordinary – this memoir of growing up in Kashmir in the '90s is illuminating, heartbreaking, and beautifully told.'

— KAMILA SHAMSIE, author of *Home Fire*

'Written with aching tenderness, *Rumours of Spring* reveals the intimate details of Bashir's childhood in Kashmir and lays bare the brutal realities of Indian repression. By using the life of her family as a lens, Bashir settles an unflinching gaze on the emotional, physical and mental toll of years of oppression. This is an unforgettable work that refuses silence. It is an urgent, brave call for justice.'

— MAAZA MENGISTE, author of *The Shadow King*

'Page after page, Farah Bashir juxtaposes moments of heart-stopping terror and beauty in a stunning memoir of life and love under a bloody military occupation.'

— MIRZA WAHEED, author of *Tell Her Everything*

'An extraordinary memoir, lovingly vivid and sparklingly precise. I couldn't put it down, and even after it had ended, the people and their stories – wonderful, horrific, familiar and unfathomable – stayed textured and formidable in my mind.'

— JENNIFER CROFT, author of *Homesick*

'A beautifully tender and often heart-stopping memoir of growing up in a world that is spinning out of control.'

— MAHESH RAO, author of *Polite Society*

RUMOURS OF SPRING

A Girlhood in Kashmir

FARAH BASHIR

FOURTH ESTATE · *New Delhi*

First published in India in hardback in 2021 by Fourth Estate
An imprint of HarperCollins *Publishers*
A-75, Sector 57, Noida, Uttar Pradesh 201301, India
www.harpercollins.co.in

Copyright © Farah Bashir 2021

P-ISBN: 978-93-5422-421-8
E-ISBN: 978-93-5422-422-5

The views and opinions expressed in this book are the author's own and the facts are as reported by her, and the publishers are not in any way liable for the same.

Farah Bashir asserts the moral right
to be identified as the author of this work.

All rights reserved. No part of this publication may be reproduced, stored in a retrieval system, or transmitted, in any form or by any means, electronic, mechanical, photocopying, recording or otherwise, without the prior permission of the publishers.

Typeset in 11.5/15.2 Arno Pro at
Manipal Technologies Limited, Manipal

Printed and bound at
Thomson Press (India) Ltd

This book is produced from independently certified FSC™ paper
to ensure responsible forest management.

For the children of Kashmir, who know nothing of a normal childhood
For my grandmother, Sarwa
For my sister, Bushera

Sing, daughters, of one woman and one thousand, of those multitudes who rushed like wind to free a country from poisonous beasts. Sing, children of those who came before you, of those who laid the path on which you tread toward warmer suns.
...
Sing of those who are no more,
Sing of the giants still amongst you,
Sing of those yet to be born.
Sing.

from *The Shadow King* by Maaza Mengiste

CONTENTS

EVENING

The Day I Was Dead	3
Memory of the Scalp	13
Do Wishes Come True?	18
Evening Salute	22
The Metallic Monster	28
Rituals Old and New	34

NIGHT

When Our Folk Tales Dried Up	45
Heart Goes Boom-Boom	50
May I Become Invisible, Please?	55
The Country with a Burnt Post Office	60
Period Pangs and a Stray Bullet	70
Djinn and Jahanam	74

EARLY HOURS

Roll Call	83
Pasikdar: The Benign Spirit	89
The Door on the Floor	93
I Miss Walking	100

DAWN

Forbidden Courtyard	109
Surah Fheel: Faith in the Faith	115
I Would Grow Up to Be Collateral Damage	120
Shadow of a Siege	125
Cinemas? No Scope!	130
A Wedding, a Funeral	135

MORNING

Speech Impediments	143
Curfew as Poison	148
Memory of the Lake	153
Shared Grief	160
Of Men, Mice and Violence	165
Tiny Knots of Faith	171

AFTERLIFE

Q. K.: The Courtyard Graffiti	177
The Saintless	181
The Attic and the Sieve	186
Sounds and the Silencer	190
Games Our Children Play	197
The Dread of Dastarkhwaan	200
The Attested Dead	206

Notes	213
Acknowledgements	227

EVENING

THE DAY I WAS DEAD

IT WAS A CHILLY DECEMBER evening in 1994, which had the stillness of snow without any snow.

I had turned eighteen that year, and for the first time in my life, I felt grateful for the dusk-to-dawn curfew. My grandmother, Bobeh, had died late that afternoon. It was because of the curfew that I could spend an extra night with her around. On an ordinary night, curfew swelled up the air with fear and uncertainty. It controlled everything. It disciplined people inside their own houses, animals on the streets, and had even tamed the loud sneezes of the tobacco-seller who lived two houses from ours. That night, however, the curfew felt like a blessing.

I didn't get to say a proper goodbye to my grandmother, my Bobeh. Had I known on the night of 18 December that it would be our last one together, I'd have been more polite to her. The next day, she was already gone by the time I reached home after taking my exams.

The previous night, I had decided to stay up late to study. Bobeh stayed up with me as long as the dim light of the kerosene lamp lasted. She'd had an asthmatic attack recently, and that made her look visibly distressed. But it was her unwavering gaze on me that made me irritable.

'I *am* studying! Do you think I'll revise insincerely if you look away?' I told her, raising both my chemistry book and my voice.

She didn't respond, but continued to watch me, wheezing occasionally. She had had several asthmatic attacks before, but they had become more frequent since the time the firing of tear gas had become the norm. It used to be so harsh on her. Later I wondered if, on that night, it was also the torment of death that had shown on her face.

In the morning, after I had left to take the exam, a few adjoining neighbourhoods between home and school were cordoned off by the troops so that they could conduct search operations, commonly known as 'crackdown'. On such days, our roll number slips doubled as our identity passes and we were let through. By the time we finished writing our exam, at around two o'clock, the search had been extended to more areas. By the time I reached home, it was around five.

Chemistry was the first paper on the schedule. I had done reasonably well and the feeling of relief that followed gave me a ravenous appetite. As always, I had been too nervous that morning to eat anything and had sat through my exam on an empty stomach. I was looking forward to a hearty meal, but the detour I had to take emaciated me further. Famished, I reached home to find a commotion of people outside our koche. My heart sank.

Was someone hit by a bullet?
Who could it be?
Was Father injured at the shop?
Was Mother hit by a grenade shell or a shrapnel?

As these thoughts came to my mind, my throat tightened, as if I was being strangled. I could barely breathe. I inched towards our house with wobbly knees. The main wooden door was open. A couple of shopkeepers from the neighbourhood were coming out of the house as I floated in bewildered. Sajida, our elderly next door neighbour, and the keeper of most secrets in the neighbourhood, was descending the stairs as I slowly climbed up. 'Go, have one last look at your grandmother.' As Sajida uttered those words, for a brief second, all I could see around me was a blackness. The turquoise shawl she had wrapped around her head disappeared. The darkness was followed by a sharp pain in my belly. I got my period which lasted less than a day.

In the corridor, I heard Father's voice say: 'How am I to take the responsibility of so many curfew passes? What if they shoot someone?'

They were trying to decide if they should bury Bobeh that very night or on the following day. Father seemed adamant about everyone's safety. He declared that the burial was to be postponed by a night.

Father, Mother, Ramzan Kaak and Pophtaeth, an aunt of mine who had come to pay Bobeh a visit, stayed up all night in the living room as some of the neighbours left. They spent the long hours praying for her. I didn't pray. I felt numb, and then restless.

That night, too, the room was dimly lit. Mother had arranged blankets under which everyone could sit through the night. Ramzan Kaak readied kerosene lamps and lined them by the door. Everyone had a booklet of Quran that they were reciting verses from. Had the body of Bobeh not been lying in the corner where she'd usually sit, it could pass off as the Night of Atonement or Shab-e-Baraat, when all of us stayed up the whole night to pray. The room was humming, but a strange silence befell the corner Bobeh was lying in. The heavy soundlessness of that corner was more overwhelming than the unease the silence of the dawn-to-dusk curfew brought on. I sat in another corner of the room, staring at Bobeh's still hands and her long, delicate fingers.

There was a night when Bobeh looked close to how she looked after passing. Pale, silent and stiffened. It was on the eve of Eid in 1989, the Eid that set a precedence for future ones to come. That Eid eve, as a twelve-year-old girl, I decided unwittingly to never participate in festivities again. In fact, from then on, I began associating inexplicable melancholy with Eid, and the heaviness that settled on the heart that day sank deeper each year.

Before 1989, my anticipation of the festivities on the eve of Eid usually surpassed the excitement I felt during the festival itself. There was an eagerness to wear new clothes, along with matching shoes and fashionable accessories. The rich, spicy aromas that wafted from every kitchen in the neighbourhood, suffused not just the individual courtyards but the entire mesh of interconnected narrow streets. The menu at our house was carefully selected. Mother would cook some of the dishes herself while the rest were ordered from Ashraf waze, the renowned chef of our area. Father would sit quietly in a corner of the living room, away from his usual spot. With his back towards the door, he'd stealthily count the crisp currency notes that he'd distribute among his sisters and their children as Eidi the next day. The whole evening would be punctuated with the sound of the main door being opened and shut by my sister Hina, who'd invariably have to go out for her last-minute visits to the tailor and the salon.

In comparison, the day of Eid was rather muted. It began with wearing fineries, sitting in front of the Dastarkhwaan, drinking kahwe, breaking bread together as a family. The rest of the day was spent waiting for the relatives to visit our house with my share of Eidi.

When I was around eight or nine years old, Father would pack me in the back of his car – an ochre Range Rover, JKD 7575 – on Eid as he'd drive along with Ramzan Kaak. Ramzan Kaak was Father's assistant at his clothing shop in Boher Kadal. He was roughly Father's age, physically stronger, and the most trusted man of our household. I remember seeing the mass prayer congregation that year at Eid Gah where hundreds of men, clad in crisp Khan dress and skull caps, had gathered to pray with their children, who were dressed up in bright colours. Rows of vendors selling wooden horse carts, rattlers, red strips of crackers and colourful plastic toys surrounded the large field where the men prayed. I didn't know then that the same prayer-ground would come to be known as the martyrs' graveyard.

I was never attracted to toys, and that was perhaps because I wanted to do the things my beautiful sister, Hina, did. A decade elder to me, she was past her age of playing with dolls and so, I, too, didn't develop a liking towards them. In fact, that year (1989), as I turned twelve, I was finally allowed to take the first step in emulating Hina's ways. After much bargaining with and emotionally blackmailing Mother, I could visit the salon that Hina used to frequent. Moving up from the barber who used to cut Father's hair at home to the hairdresser famous for styling fashionable cuts, felt like a rite of passage for me. The occasion chosen for that was Eid. No one said no. But the yes was delayed interminably.

The salon, where some of my friends had already been for their grown-up haircuts, was in the posh neighbourhood of Raj Bagh. As per my sister's advice, we scheduled the salon visit for the evening so that our coiffure would retain their shapes the next morning. I felt very glamorous in my freshly trimmed, salon-washed, blow-dried hair. I felt like the model from a shampoo ad who turned her head from left to right and right to left as she flaunted her straight, lustrous, bouncy hair. '*Halo giiiiiiiiirl,*' the jingle played in the background as she looked happy and confident with her lush hair.

We were among the last few customers at the salon. By the time we left, it was already dark, but we noticed a marked shift in the air which had nothing to do with the inky, funereal colour of the evening sky. Shopkeepers were bringing down the store shutters in a frenzy. Instead of the pre-Eid festive chaos caused by the shoppers and shopkeepers alike, the roads began emptying out. There was barely any traffic. Police vehicles were whizzing past us and there were policemen all around.

'Looks like a curfew. Like we're under Gul Karfi again,' Hina whispered to me. 'Hold my hand and don't look up.'

I clutched Hina's wrist, and feverishly wished that we'd somehow vanish from the streets and land straight into our living room with Father, Mother and Bobeh. I could feel the tears pooling in my eyes, but the tears just wouldn't roll down. Perhaps it had something to do with the panic that was building up inside me.

Home was some distance from the salon and we had to break our journey into two halves. We took a minibus until Amira Kadal and managed to negotiate the second leg of the journey with an autorickshaw driver who sensed our desperation and didn't charge us for the ride. He dropped us in Nawab Bazar, around a kilometre away from our house.

'*Yath tcha nih patah kith haalat roazan.* Can't say how the circumstances will shape up.' With that, he drove his autorickshaw off, like a bullet, as they say.

As we took a few steps forward, a police jeep was doing rounds and announced a message in loop in as hostile a manner as possible: '*Awaam se* appeal *ki jaati hai ki apne gharoon se baahar na nikleyn, sheher mein* shoot at sight *ka* order *hai*. People are requested not to step outside their homes for there is shoot at sight order across the city.'

Hina urged me to walk faster. I cannot recall with certainty, but perhaps I was slowing down to look at the shards of glass and plastic scattered on the road. Amidst broken lamps, coloured glass bangles, stomped-on plastic kitchen sets, dolls with soiled and squished faces, there was debris enough to distract one all along the way. We reached home after walking for what seemed like an eternity and arrived to Bobeh's sobs.

Our legs having transformed into trembling, rickety appendages, Hina and I dragged ourselves up the stone steps leading to the living room. We could hear the phone ring incessantly and grew more anxious because of that. Bobeh sat beside it, oblivious to the noise and panic that it was creating. A map of purple lines appeared on her temples as her *daej*, the embroidered, square bandana, with which she covered her hair, lay crumpled on the floor. She was breathing laboriously; her asthma seemed to have worsened. The moment she saw us, she held her uncovered head in her hands. Even in the moment of panic, my brain registered what an uncommon sight it was.

'Are you really alive?'

Bobeh repeated her question in a broken voice as she held my face in her ice-cold hands. While my face was still in her corpse-like hands, I pulled away from her, as if someone had pushed me. I could hear my heart beat loudly and felt my body shake.

I was in a daze, hardly being able to take note of what was happening. Mother walked into the room and held us close to her. She asked us questions, most of which were answered by Hina. I cannot remember where Father was. I heard his voice coming faintly from the direction of the courtyard of his cousin, the one who lived next door. The phone kept ringing. Someone, possibly Ramzan Kaak, finally picked up the phone and said, 'Shukur, she's here, they're safe.'

Mother said that all our relatives were calling to ask after me. There was news that a twelve-year-old from our clan had been killed. Asiya, one of my friends from school, who lived nearby, had been calling, as she too had feared that it was me. Neither Bobeh nor anyone else could confirm anything until they saw me in flesh. Unbeknownst to us at the time, my second cousin, exactly my age, had also gone out with his father. They had been out to buy shoes for him for Eid. As they were returning home in their car, he was hit by a bullet. His last words to his father were, '*Myeha log haelyis toat*. I am feeling warm on the side of my stomach.' He bled to death on his way to the hospital.

At that point, no one knew what exactly had happened. Ramzan Kaak came to the room and said that there was news of multiple shootings, and the city was under curfew. Barely a kilometre from where our house was, next to Father's shop in Boher Kadal, there was a shooting incident involving a well-known militant, Mushtaq Latram. Absorbing the news from all around made my hands shake. In a moment of confusion and fear, I plucked a chunk of my hair from right behind my ear. It hurt to pull the hair out, but my hands needed to clutch at something. I pulled some out again to punish myself for not being able to make sense of what had befallen us as a people. I couldn't help but feel that none of this would have happened had I not troubled everyone about going to the salon. Somehow, I felt responsible for all of it: for being rumoured to be dead, for Bobeh's condition: she had begun to wheeze uncontrollably. Since then, a dark, silent cloud of death hovers above me every Eid.

MEMORY OF THE SCALP

TAKING CARE OF MY HAIR was my grandmother's favourite activity until I shied away from it. '*Muss gov korri hund vass,*' she would say while massaging my scalp, reminding me that hair is the best ornament a girl can have. Bobeh held sections of my hair carefully between her palms and applied her magic potion right from the root to the tip of each strand. Seemaab dissolved in ghyev was the potion that she so painstakingly prepared to keep my hair free from lice infestations. Every alternate Friday evening, upon her instructions, Ramzan Kaak brought home two vials containing tiny globules of seemaab to her.

She'd spend at least an hour the following morning patiently dissolving the slithery mercury into homemade ghyev. She'd grease the palm of her left hand with some of the clarified butter and calmly rub the mercury with the thumb of her right hand. Her hands would move to an inaudible rhythm even as the rest of her body remained still. She would murmur wanwun, just like I had seen some carpet weavers do, mysteriously working their fingers and making masterpieces while humming taeleem.

'Maam Toath used to apply it to my scalp in the same way. That's why my hair is still thick after so many years. He would ask me to be still on the braandh and generously apply the mixture to my scalp,' Bobeh would reminisce as she'd sit me down in front of her while applying the concoction.

I suppose that was her way of reliving her childhood, being nostalgic about as much motherly care as she could garner in her memories.

She had lost her mother soon after she was born. Thereafter, her father had refused to look at her, and so her maternal uncle took care of her. She had lived with him until the age of eleven; that was when she was married off to my grandfather as his second wife. My grandfather's first wife could not bear him children, so he married a younger girl, my grandmother, who bore him many. The two wives lived in harmony in the same house until the older one died of measles.

I relished my grandmother's pampering and never protested her applying the tonic to my hair. I preferred that to the emulsion that my mother applied to her hair. Mother made a paste from mustard oil and yoghurt, which had a pungent odour that I disliked. Since everything at home – from yakhen to zombre thool – was cooked in mustard oil, its slightest aroma reminded me of Mother's unwashed hair.

After applying seemaab and ghyev, Bobeh tied my hair in a neat, tight plait. I was allowed to wash it off the next day. At night, so as not to soil the pillowcase, I'd be given an old piece of cloth which I tied around my hair like a bandana. In summer, I would look forward to the long, Sunday-morning showers. After shampooing my hair, I'd chase the sun from window to window, or step outside into the courtyard to let it fluff up my well-cared for wavy, auburn hair. In winter, for the lack of sun, Bobeh would wrap my head in her embroidered raffal shawls to keep chill at bay.

None of that happened that year. All the care ended in the winter of 1990. Not due to the unavailability of seemaab. I suppose it was still stocked up, maybe even rotting, in the shops which remained mostly shut because of the unending periods of curfew. Following the autumn of 1989, I did not let Bobeh touch my scalp or caress my hair.

Our five-storeyed house stood on one of the busiest streets of Shehr-e-Khaas, the old quarters of the city, where absolute silence was rare, even in the dead of the night. But the curfew nights were different. The imposition of night curfew added an eerie silence to the darkness. They weren't just silent, but full of fear. The gunshots sounded louder, the screams more vivid, and the engines of jeeps patrolling on the streets and

Zaene Kadal, the bridge over the silently flowing Jhelum, made frightening noises.

I found it difficult to fall asleep in that silence.

While I'd be trying to escape its eeriness and locate a familiar sound to fall asleep to, I'd constantly fiddle with my hair. That'd get their roots into a twist. A little bump, the size of a pimple, would form at the base of the strands. That little bump would swell up to the size of a walnut over the next few minutes with a strange burning sensation and a throbbing pain, one that would last the whole night. To soothe the spot, I'd half-pull the strands. Without much effort, they'd come out like hot needles from my scalp. I'd hold each strand between the thumb and index finger, and place my middle finger slightly above them, and with one violent jerk I'd root out the strand. The movement felt pleasurable, but intensified the pain. Weak from the irritation the strands would eventually come out with a slight shake but a sharp sting. I'd forget about the outside eeriness as I'd be too engrossed trying to soothe my hurting and burning scalp by pulling my hair out for hours. I'd lose track of time. Sometimes, I'd forcefully pluck out a chunk of hair trying to get rid of any possibility of hurting myself further, but the pain persisted. Every night, pain found a different spot. It travelled. On the crown, above the ears, near the temples, above the nape, that is where it hurt the most … almost everywhere. It travelled across my whole head.

Some mornings, I found tiny beads of dried blood on the bald spots that I'd created overnight. Some nights, when I didn't pluck too many strands, I'd keep caressing and pressing the tender, hairless spots to calm them. I had become so obsessed with my scalp that during the day, I'd take a pen and scratch the hairless patches to extricate the remnants of any painful membrane from the night and to cover the spots with ink. As much as I'd be occupied with it, it increasingly felt embarrassing. Often, the thought of someone discovering my new-found habit would make me irritable. I'd feel annoyed and rebellious if my grandmother made a mention of massaging my scalp in passing. It felt like someone was stripping me bare. During the day, when my scalp began to show or shine, I'd cover my head with a floral scarf. By night, fluffy balls of my thick strands started to gather and float next to my bed. I'd feel remorseful in the mornings, but at night, it got me through the fear-filled sleeplessness. If I ever heard a knock, a wail, or gunshots, I would hurriedly and mercilessly jerk out one strand after another. Come morning, I didn't want anyone to see my hair gone and bald patches appear.

DO WISHES COME TRUE?

'WISH THERE IS A CURFEW tomorrow in the day, so that we can keep Bobeh home for one more day...' I caught myself thinking a terrible thought that winter night in 1994.

Then I heard a voice inside my head censuring me: *'Be careful what you wish for. Especially during a moment of Saat-e-Hassan. Your wish – good or bad – can come true.'*

Bobeh had her ways of reprimanding. It was mostly indirect. She'd instil fear to make us feel responsible for our words and actions. Sometimes, she'd say that if we led a life that was pious and free from malice towards others, the chances of us meeting Khawaja Khazir were high. 'But we need to be innately pure – free from takabur, not engaging in gossiping, lying and cheating – to recognize the benevolent being,' she would add, ensuring we didn't get too hopeful about the meeting.

I must admit that I believed I'd come across Khawaja Khazir someday in person. I even asked Bobeh for the physical characteristics that could help me recognize him. She said I'd get to know once I shook hands with him because he had a bone missing at the base of his right thumb. After registering that piece of crucial information, for a long time, whenever I had an opportunity to shake hands with anyone, rare for a twelve-year-old, I would be thoroughly disappointed to find all the bones intact in the other person's hand. But I continued to observe people's hands intently for several years. Until the meeting would happen, there was something changing in me. I was beginning to be more careful in choosing my words lest they came true. I was becoming a little paranoid about my thoughts too.

Growing up, as far as I can remember, I'd always wanted the winter vacation to be prolonged by a month or so. So, after the winter of 1990, when the schools did not reopen until May and we could not resume classes after the three-month long vacation, Bobeh's words rang truer than ever. Her reproach for words uttered irresponsibly made me feel guilty for the extended but unwanted vacation. Sometimes I'd think it was all my fault for having casually wished for something that had turned irrevocably real.

Our school's winter vacation started around mid-December and ended around the first week of March. The icy landscape had thawed by then, but for the snow to completely melt away and make way for spring when the air would be less chilly and more pleasant, it would be a month-long wait. March was just an in-between damp month, filled with the sound of drizzle, and the part-harsh, part-soothing music of the occasional heavy downpour on the slanting tin roofs of our home. The mornings were ideal for sleeping in and waking up early to attend school felt rather cruel. Winter, on its way out, cast an unending sense of foreboding. To expect change in the season in a month's time felt less like a reality but more like rumours of spring.

The snow that hardened during Chillai Kalan, forty days of bitter cold starting with the solstice, lined the sides of the narrow streets and by-lanes, especially those of Shehr-e-Khaas; the rain turned it into slush. The roads looked like large canvases of abstract art. Stripes of geometric patterns formed on grey slush – impressions from fat tyres of cars and 1-Ton army trucks, and thin bicycle wheels, and irregular imprints from varying shoe sizes and boots. While there was the usual fear of slipping on such risky stretches, I had a bigger concern. It was to remove the clusters of little specks of mud that formed at the back of the shalwar of our white school uniform.

Washing and drying the thick spun fabric overnight was nearly impossible. Sometimes, after having been laid out to dry for two days, when the uniform was still damp, Bobeh would use her kanger to dry the wet parts. It could take up to a few hours. Then, Ramzan Kaak would prepare the heavy iron filled with hot coals to press out any remaining moisture floating like mist over the uniform.

I preferred our primary school winter wear – green trousers made of polyester-based material. Mud stains could be easily brushed off from it once they had dried. After a round of sturdy brushing with a coat brush, which came in a silver case that had been a part of Mother's dowry, the green trousers were good to be worn for at least two more days. But the change to white in high school created additional stress. Some stains, even after being scrubbed off, left behind a ghostly grey shadow. Somedays, I'd wish for our uniform to be changed into the camouflage print of the troops. Neither mud nor bloodstains show on camouflage. 'How lucky are the ones who wear it,' I'd think, but was quick enough to dismiss the thought. I'd shudder as I remembered my grandmother's warning about wishes coming true.

EVENING SALUTE

BOBEH SPENT HOURS ON THE second floor, sitting behind different windows. In the mornings, behind the wire mesh of the window in the kitchen, she watched me leave for the bus stop with Ramzan Kaak. During late afternoons, when I returned from the school, I'd find my favourite hung-yoghurt hanging in a white muslin cloth, from a peg above the same window. In the evenings, she would soak up the charm of the street as it filled with young women returning from colleges or tuitions, and men gathered at waan pyend discussing politics or bantering.

Bobeh used windows for another purpose. She communicated with her youngest and favourite daughter, Nelofar – a lecturer at a nearby college – through different windows, as she didn't rely on the phone too much.

Bobeh would stand near the window of the drawing room if she had an urgent message to pass on. It was the corner window, the first one visible from the lane which led to my aunt's college. She made it appear urgent by standing there, for this would prompt my aunt to walk into our house immediately. Some days, to kill time, she sat on the windowsill of the study adjacent to the drawing room. My sister Hina also used windows to call her friend Rifat. Her window was on the second floor, in our parents' room, which was right above the living room. On some summer evenings before 1989, after school, I'd spend time by the windows of the big hall on the fourth floor of our house. I'd take a bottle of water with me and empty it slowly by pouring it on to the street. It amused me to see the droplets dance on their way down. The water never fell on anyone. Or maybe it did. But no one ever looked up in anger to reprimand me. Every window in our house seemed to have been assigned a specific role, each one had numerous tales to tell.

Because of Bobeh, the windows of our house remained slightly open even during the harshest of winters. Being asthmatic, she needed a constant flow of fresh air. But that seemed to be more of an excuse, as she couldn't rid herself of the habit to peer outside and observe passers-by. It was as if through them, she were living an active life, since she hardly went out herself. However, things changed after 1989 and the windows had to be tightly shut during the incessant spells of curfew.

In the late autumn of 1990, it had already been three seasons since we had opened the windows, especially the ones overlooking the street. Open windows were an easy and unobstructed passage for bullets and grenade splinters to make their way inside. Even a peep could be dangerous. Letting in fresh air could cost us dearly. Those solid wooden planks also helped keep the smoke from tear gas at bay. Whenever there were protests, which was sometimes a few times a day in our part of the town, people turned out in large numbers chanting, '*Ham kya chahte? Azadi!*' Fearing the juloos would swell up with more protestors, the troops, apart from firing bullets, fired tear gas shells on to the gatherings. The bluish air would irritate our noses, and sting our eyes and throats, even when we were indoors. We learnt to keep a wet cloth handy or washed our faces with cold water to make it less annoying, less painful.

Bobeh, however, was affected the most and in the worst ways. Her asthma worsened at the slightest hint of smoke. Even when Mother used extra chilli while cooking, Bobeh would start wheezing in the next room, her face changing colour. As sturdy as she was on the outside, she had fragile lungs. For years, she had been a smoker. Smoking jajeer a few times a day had been habitual of her, and Mother too would steal a few puffs from her hookah. Eventually, as the lung infection nearly consumed her life, Bobeh had to quit smoking. Little did she know, the infection and the fragility would return. Those inescapable blue fumes from tear gas shells crept indoors through closed windows and held her lungs hostage.

Then, a particular window began to puzzle us. This was the street-facing one in the study. For a week, at around six o'clock each evening, it stood mysteriously ajar. On each occasion, it was left unbolted, evidence enough to confirm that someone had tried to open it or hadn't cared to shut it securely after opening it.

Mother offered an esoteric explanation. 'Maybe the birds are trying to say something. We don't leave crumbs outside on the sill anymore in the evenings, as it is patrol time. They must be going hungry. Perhaps a bird-spirit is reminding us to feed them.' She would then utter '*Nezabaen sunnd tchu bozan Khodah*' with utmost authority and no one countered with that lofty logic that there may be a mysterious power in the powerless.

We waited in anticipation; perhaps we'd discover that the window had become someone's obsession. On most of the days when there was a curfew or a hartal (civil curfew), Father, since he couldn't regularly run his business at the shop, either slept endlessly or re-read newspapers to kill his time. He also developed a new habit of checking the bolts all over our house in the afternoons and again, slightly before dusk, just when the night curfew was imposed. In fact, everyone had cultivated some new personal quirk around that time. Although it had been almost a year, none of us had accepted the night curfew yet. We tried to distract ourselves before the routine lockdown started. Earlier, it used to be the liveliest time of the day in our neighbourhood. Its shift to being funereal didn't make sense.

I had developed an urge to relieve myself at dusk. During one of the routine trips to the toilet, I chanced upon Father's elder sister, Pophtaeth, in the study.

I was curious to see what she would do as she neared the window. I wanted to be the one to have solved the mystery of the tampered window bolts. I stood still, watching her as she perched herself on the little seating area next to the window. The window was unbolted and ajar. Slowly, she lifted her hand and dropped it a few times. Her gaze was fixed outdoors, on the street, at something that I couldn't see from where I was standing. But I knew that it was the hour of armed patrol by the troops who marched past our house every evening. She lifted her hand again, meekly this time, to her forehead. Saluting with a fearful face and a half-sprouted smile, she looked like a child trying to appease the playground bully. I chuckled to myself. Oblivious of my presence, she repeated the 'salute' a couple of times. I found it hilarious. A few minutes later, as she walked into the living room, I burst into laughter. Father was poring over an old newspaper. I was excited to narrate how Pophtaeth had been saluting the patrolling party.

I had expected him to be amused as well as be proud of me for solving the mystery of the open window. Before he could react, or anyone could ask Pophtaeth questions, she blurted out guiltily, 'I thought next time there is a search operation or an encounter in the neighbourhood, the troops would show some mercy. *Myeha dop tyim karan raham.* Maybe they'll remember that someone from this house saluted them.' Pophtaeth had come to stay with us for a few days after she had lost her house to a fire that had engulfed her neighbourhood in Kawdoar. After the gun-battle between militants and paramilitary forces, the troops blew up the site of encounter by setting fire to it. The fire spread to the adjoining houses in the congested neighbourhood.

Two storeys of her house were up in flames, and the rest of it was inundated with a deluge caused by extinguishers. Her neighbours couldn't recover anything.

Father didn't react. His gaze had moved from the newspaper to his empty teacup.

On the evening of 19 December 1994, the same aunt was the only relative to be present when Bobeh passed away. I wondered if she'd sit by the same window when they'd take my grandmother's coffin for burial the next day.

THE METALLIC MONSTER

AT HOME, ALL SIX OF us had our designated corners in the living room.

If you entered through the main door, you'd find Father sitting opposite the entrance. To his right sat Mother with her back to the kitchen, yet close enough to its side door lest she needed to attend to anything urgently. To Father's left sat Hina. Diagonally opposite to Father was where Bobeh used to sit, in a corner that overlooked the pebbled courtyard. Next to her and opposite Father, sat Ramzan Kaak. I sat in the middle of the room in front of my grandmother.

That night, she lay in her designated corner. I sat where Hina used to sit.

Our winter evenings in the 1980s replicated themselves throughout the decade until 1989. The routine was that Father would shut his shop earlier than he did in the summer. He'd be home at around 8.30 on dry nights, but walked back earlier when it snowed. Habitually, he'd light a cigarette as he read newspapers or went through his ledger books. On some evenings, he and Ramzan Kaak would recount funny incidents that they had witnessed at the shop during the day. Sometimes, they'd narrate an old one and laugh over it again with the newness of the first time. There were a couple of those 'classic' ones that neither Father nor Ramzan Kaak seemed to tire of.

'When Miseh Laal ran after his "train of plates" and landed on that tray, remember how it went sliding through the street!' The story somehow sounded funnier with every retelling. The two grown men would laugh so hard that only they could understand what they'd mumble in their hysterical bouts.

Bobeh also chuckled along, while untangling huge yarn balls for Mother and Hina's knitting and crochet projects. She moved her hands gracefully and made the entire chore look meditative. She used two bags to ready the yarn: one was for immediate use and another for later. She untangled the set, meant for later, wrapped it around her undulating knees, as if in a trance. She twisted multiple skeins out of it. Some were the same colour, some in mixed colours. She hummed wanwun to the movements.

Laalan tchu kormut BA/ BT
Haariy kor invarsity saal
...
Dass kad nebar tchai qabeel daeri
Tcze hav tchi saeri tamahdaar

The set of yarn balls meant for later use, she calmly wrapped around her thumb and index finger, and made mammoth bullet skeins out of it. Sometimes, Mother gave her old, knitted sweaters which Bobeh unravelled so that the yarn could be reused. Bobeh's corner of the living room would be full of colour and warmth even during the grey winters.

Hina, when she wasn't reading magazines, *Shamah* and *Pakeezah*, would sit with me and we'd fill our corner of the living room with board games such as carrom that stretched for hours. We screamed with excitement during a strike-and-pocket and yelped each time we missed it. Not to mention, we'd cheer loudly upon landing ourselves the coveted prize of the game, the burgundy queen, which stands out among the dark and light disks.

After Hina got married in a small ceremony in 1990, I lost my carrom partner. Unwittingly, I switched to sketching at the back of my notebooks. I enjoyed it. When Bobeh caught me doing so, she would prohibit me from drawing faces.

'Will you be able to bring them to life on the day of Qayamat? Why're you trying to match the creator? Nauzubillah!'

Slightly scared that I'd really be asked to bring my drawings to life on the day of judgement, I started sketching the backs of men and women. Women with long plaits, women with short hair, some wearing skirts and some in shalwar kameez, as well as the backs of lanky men (like my father) and men with broad shoulders. Though I was apprehensive that Bobeh would scold me for drawing men and ask me to stick to the good, old landscapes that I drew as a child, she did not seem to mind. So long as there were no faces, I could keep sketching.

Then one winter, no evening resembled the other except for the curfew. It began with the winter of 1990, which was not just dark but dreary. It was also the harbinger of the drearier ones to come. A horrific silence fell over our houses and our hearts. Father's sitting posture changed too. Normally, he would sit back relaxed against a large cushion which had a Chinar leaf embroidered on it; he rested his elbow on a bolster next to it, smoking his cigarettes at leisure while reading newspapers or attending to his daily ledger. Almost like a royal, I'd think. Since the winter of 1990, he began crouching, as if always in a hurry and almost ready to get up. Perhaps he was trying to curb the restlessness within him. Sometimes, he squatted and moved back and forth in a strange manner. It made me uneasy. Bobeh occasionally spun yarn skeins, but no longer hummed wanwun. Her songs disappeared. One day, she said that wanwun belonged to the funerals of young men now rather than to the weddings. I continued making sketches, but my pages were taken over by drawings of guns, spools of barbed wire and helmets of the soldiers that I sometimes caught a glimpse of during their evening patrol. During the evenings that I didn't sketch, I pulled my hair out, sometimes stealthily, sometimes openly, without caring much about being scolded or inviting glances from everyone, especially Bobeh.

'I've told you so many times not to touch your hair!'

'It's my hair, I'd...'

Before I could complete the sentence and disrespect her further by talking back, Ramzan Kaak, who was helping Mother with ironing winter clothing with a heavy coal iron, intervened. He apologized on my behalf: '*Hye wayn hez karrini dubareh, diss hez maefi.*'

Ramzan Kaak was always an amiable mediator to sort out differences between different members of the family; I had never seen him in a bad mood. In the winter of 1993, he was attacked and after that, he too changed.

It was an ordinary winter evening. After the night curfew was imposed, Ramzan Kaak went downstairs to bolt the main gate as he did every evening. That was the part of his evening chores while Father ensured that the windows and doors inside the house were securely bolted. As per routine, he went downstairs. Within seconds of his being gone, we panicked as we heard him scream: '*Ha Khodaayo, mornasa!*'

Expecting the worst, Father rushed downstairs while the rest of us froze in fear. A few minutes later, he came in carrying the burly figure of Ramzan Kaak on his back. Ramzan Kaak had been assaulted, his face and neck bleeding from violent scratch marks. His kantopi was missing and the collar of his pheran was ripped. An exceptionally strong man otherwise, Ramzan Kaak appeared to have shrunk that night. His lips were parched and his face had lost colour. Mother brought him a glass of water. We switched on all the lights to examine his injuries. The room felt so oddly lit up. Luckily, the scratches seemed superficial and home first aid sufficed.

Ramzan Kaak had been attacked by a steel monster. A faceless, steel-armour clad person, locally known as 'steel daen', had been attacking and clawing people across the city after dark.

'As if it was waiting for me! As soon as I opened the door to firmly bolt it shut, it pushed through! It had been hiding there. I turned around to run back inside the house, but it caught hold of my throat. *Shukur Khodayas kun*, it is winter and it could only tear my clothes off. Imagine if it were summer, the thing could have ripped my body open! I think some Malaik saved me and gave me the courage to scream for help!' Ramzan Kaak recounted the horrific incident, whimpering. For days, he kept his face inside the neckline of his pheran, as if hiding from another assault.

A few nights later, we were alerted by a strange, sonorous sound coming from a distant neighbourhood. It echoed eerily. We had no idea what was going on. The next day, we found out that someone else had been attacked by the steel daen in the same way Ramzan Kaak was. But then, too much fear can catapult itself into fearlessness. The people from that neighbourhood had countered the attack by creating a ruckus with metal sounds. Since the monster was shielded with metal, could it understand the language of metallic sounds?

As reports of a few more incidents began to filter in from various localities, people decided to brave chilly nights, embrace the fear of night curfew and drive out the daen. Occasionally, as night fell, we started clanging all things made of metal at our house too. We'd open our windows, strike pots against pans, and bang steel glasses and copper bowls against each other to create a warning symphony. The entire neighbourhood resounded with a steely cacophony of resistance. The monster finally disappeared.

RITUALS OLD AND NEW

THE PHONE RANG WITH A shrill sound that pierced the silence of the living room.

'*Trath yath*,' said Mother, reminding me how she had started cursing reflexively each time the phone rang in the evenings since 1989.

This time, it was my sister Hina who had called, and Mother informed her about the postponement of our grandmother's burial. While they continued the conversation, my mind drifted.

Once, in the winter of 1991, the phone had rung to coincide exactly with the 5.30 patrol. The dreadful rhythm of jackboots echoed through the bitter cold winter evenings. We did everything we could to shut the sinister, synchronized sound out. We put up heavy crewel curtains with thick linings and added a layer of woollen blankets on the latticed wooden windows, but even that did not stop the unwanted entry of those steps which pushed further, inch upon inch, into our kitchen which overlooked the street. From there, they stomped on our temples and finally entered our heads. The marching seeped into our silences, punctuated our conversations with pauses, which, in turn, jumbled our thoughts and our language.

During the hour of the evening patrol, Mother never looked at me. Never made eye-contact. She had begun arranging her silent chores around the patrol; wrapping up all the kitchen work by five o'clock so that no noise from our house reached the armed troops. Like most of us, she too had created rituals that helped her through the patrol hour: she rested her feet on a kanger, and buried her head into the ample neckline of her pheran, as if retracting into her own womb. The living room too changed into a different space at that hour, with all its lights dimmed.

And then the phone rang.

'*Trath yath*,' Mother muttered.

It felt like a miracle when our phone lines worked. Mother made the most of such opportunities, dialling the numbers of as many relatives as she could at those times. They did the same when their lines worked. It was no less a miracle when both lines worked at the same time.

'My headache began three days ago during the night crackdown and it hasn't left me yet. Neither has the acidity subsided. Dr Misgar has prescribed more medicines but emphasizes on the sleeping tablet to be taken at night. Even if I manage some sleep, I can't seem to get any work done during the day. I lose sleep and wakefulness both. Hello. Hello.'

Tap-tap-tap.

'You should also buy milk powder. I feel relieved after we bought two large packets. If the curfew is lifted for thirty minutes, everyone is not going to get their share. We have also bought potatoes and daal in bulk. Daal doesn't suit Bobeh though. I don't know what to cook for her. Only chicken broth and goat milk suit her, but neither are available these days. I fry potatoes. Hello? Hello. Hello.'

Tap-tap-tap.

'*Bas moklyov yi.* The line's dead.'

Mother's conversations with nearly every relative sounded the same to me. They revolved around the same things: insomnia, headaches, ration. She also assumed the same worrisome expression on her face if there was a pause from the other end of the line and in time, I learnt the words that warranted double unease, both spoken and unspoken, as she'd utter them: *byakh bunker.* Another bunker!

'But your daughters are going to walk past it every time they step out of the house. Can you not protest? What are we going to do if they put one up outside our gate as well?'

Then there was the call from Mother's relative that I eavesdropped on, along with Bobeh, whose face grew pale.

'*Haleemav Haleemav, ma vadd.* Don't cry, Haleema, don't cry,' Mother was consoling her cousin sister over the phone. Then she added in a whisper, 'I too have heard. Yes, Kunan Poshpora. *Boozum.*'

As I tried to hear what Mother said next, I couldn't shake off a strange, nauseous feeling of fear that gripped me. We had heard about the unspeakable things that happened to the women from two villages: Kunan and Poshpora. To the young and the elderly. I tried not to think too much about it as I did not want to recreate the helplessness of the women in my head. As if they hadn't gone through enough! But I couldn't stop imagining the air there, filled with funereal sounds and wails, or perhaps it was completely silent there as they tried to wrap their pain and shame in the darkness of the night ... I stopped there.

Mother hung up and murmured, 'We're lucky there's no bunker below our house. I know we have to put up with the patrolling party a few times a day, but to live in constant fear like Haleema's family is ... unimaginable.'

Haleema's house was a three-storeyed structure. They had rented a shop on the ground floor to a chicken farmer. By dint of being at one of the busiest junctions near Jama Masjid in Malaroat, the shop became an ideal place for the paramilitary to station themselves at. They threw the poultryman out for 'security reasons', obviously, and lodged themselves there in a bunker.

'Did you know that Kawoosa House, the large mansion near Haleema's house, the one that belonged to that prominent business family, has been taken over by the troops and the family has been evicted? Haleema's biggest fear is that the same is in store for every house around Jama Masjid, in and around Navyut,' Mother was telling Bobeh, who was listening quietly, wheezing occasionally and spitting phlegm into her gilded copper spittoon.

'But she must be worried about Anjum,' Bobeh said after a while, spelling out Haleema's real concern.

Anjum was around my age, slightly older, barely out of her teens. With the paramilitary moving in as their new tenants, Haleema had become paranoid about the safety of her young daughter. She locked all the doors from inside at all times, even during the day. She kept vigil at night. At the onset of insurgency, she had already sent her son out of the valley to work as a salesman for a well-off, distant relative. That'd just left the three of them in the house. Her husband, much older than her, owned a small grocery shop nearby, that he opened only when the circumstances permitted. Haleema rarely stepped out of the house and didn't let her daughter even peep out of the window. If ever she decided to go out, she made her husband shut the shop and guard their daughter. Almost all of Haleema's trips outdoors were to the nearby shrines. There she would tie votive threads, praying for the bunker below their house to be removed. She consulted pirs, who gave her holy water to sprinkle around their house, and amulets to hang from behind the windows and doors to prevent the men in uniform living below their living room from venturing upstairs.

One morning after offering Fajr, Haleema was sprinkling the house with holy water when she heard a gunshot. Assuming the worst, she looked at her husband and daughter, both of whom were sleeping in their respective beds. Later it turned out that the gunshot was fired in the bunker below. One of the troops had shot himself dead with his service rifle.

'You all keep mentioning ben-kar!' Bobeh asked innocently one day. 'What does that mean?'

'A curse,' Mother responded hurriedly as she left the room. As if by bypassing the correct definition of the word, she was negating the possibility of one being erected outside our gate.

Annoyed at the vagueness of the explanation offered, Bobeh turned to me to ask what a 'ben-kar' was.

'Bunk-er,' I said, correcting her pronunciation, 'is where the troops live. It looks like a dark room from the outside. They make it by stacking sacks filled with sand or soil, I think. Each bunker has a small, squarish opening, covered with a mesh from which the tips of rifles stick out.' Then, remembering a crucial detail, I added, 'And on the outside, the bunker is surrounded by large spools of concertina wire.'

She was startled by the detailed description I gave. She got worked up. 'Don't you know that you are not supposed to look at a soldier? You are supposed to keep your gaze lowered!'

I remained silent and did not attempt to explain that once we were outdoors, it was impossible to miss the hideous structures. Like weed, they had cropped up everywhere, they followed us no matter which route we took, they stared at us in our faces. Who knew they would eventually become landmarks and become a part of our addresses: 'the house next to the small bunker', 'the lane before the large bunker'!

Later that evening, still curious about the kind of impact the bunkers would have on our lives, my grandmother caught hold of Ramzan Kaak and asked him to tell her more. He was having his last cup of dum chai after dinner.

Ramzan Kaak said, 'Bunkers are houses of the troops. They are built according to the number of men that are to be stationed inside. Existing houses are also being turned into large bunkers. New ones are being constructed all over the city with hundreds of sandbags. Some bunkers have planted geraniums in old helmets that hang outside while others decorate theirs with empty liquor bottles.'

His description of what a bunker looked like largely matched mine. He did however add the detail of troops decorating the outside of the bunkers with liquor bottles that I had missed before being abruptly rebuked by Bobeh.

'They are everywhere: in front of our shop, next to the clinic of Dr Nasti, your ophthalmologist, next to the shrine of Shah-e-Hamdan, everywhere!' Ramzan Kaak spat out the details devoid of his usual storytelling charms.

'After all, where are these lakhs of soldiers going to live?' he added, loudly sipping dum chai from his round, handle-less, Chinese teacup. 'Amidst us, obviously. And that is where they are. Sooner or later, it will be our turn. I have heard that hotels, cinemas, some schools have all been occupied. Outside Srinagar, in the villages, they have built large camps in residential areas.

The next time I accompany you to visit the doctor, Bobeh, you shall see these bunkers for yourself,' he ended the conversation just as he picked up his cup to exit the living room to retire for the night.

'I just hope they vanish before my next visit,' Bobeh replied.

NIGHT

WHEN OUR FOLK TALES DRIED UP

BOBEH LAY UNDER A PURPLE chenille quilt. Next to the body, sat Father, reciting verses from the Quran. Mother was silently sobbing while also inspecting embers in the spare kangris, neatly lined by the door.

'Shukur, there is no load-shedding tonight. Even while leaving, she made sure she didn't cause us any inconvenience. *Moaj aes jantich hooer,*' Mother mumbled to herself and then asked me to recite prayers.

I'd heard her, but didn't pay any heed. I kept my eyes tightly shut. I was drifting away to a state between sleep and wakefulness, where the eyelids may shut the world out, but the ears hear everything. Both perceiving their own realities…

I am a middle-aged, stout woman, seated in the corridor of a dilapidated house. My face is radiant. With resilience, perhaps? My thin lips are firmly pressed against each other, my mouth drooping towards the ends, forming a broad and stretched version of the letter U, albeit inverted. It makes me appear disappointed, maybe intensely sad. The expression deepens as I hear the screams of a teenage boy coming from across a dark and dingy corridor. The clear, persistent sound of torture doesn't make me wince or tremble, though it ought to.

Amidst his shrieking, I overhear a conversation.

I hear murmurs of a young woman, but my mind is preoccupied with the screams of the teenage boy.

Moa-ji, Moa-ji.

Then the screams fade out and the conversation from next door become clearer.

The young woman says, 'I really have nothing to give you. What can I give you? I have nothing at home. I have no one to fall back on except Allah T'allah. Please help me find him. At least, tell me which prison he is in? Please.'

'You are prolonging your own misery. Do as I say and see how your life changes!'

Finally, I turn into a young woman in her teens. The sadness in her eyes makes her look decades older. She looks like someone who has endured years of suffering. Wearing an old pheran embroidered with worn-out tilleh, I am carrying a framed photograph of a young man in my halam. The face in the photograph appears smudged as if it had been recovered from a deluge. Suddenly, the framed photograph clones itself into thousands of photographs all around me, like magic, but in a scary way. There are faces of men, everywhere, but no men.

Next, I find myself sitting in a garden, blooming with long rows of daffodils. How unusual. Daffodils grow wild in graveyards. In this garden, tourists have gathered in large numbers. Men, women and children from the plains donning Kashmiri attire and jewellery, carrying wicker baskets filled with plastic flowers and ornamental bouquets, are getting photographed. They too are carrying photos in frames. Glossy prints, smiling faces. I sit there in the garden for a long time, but no one seems to notice either my presence or the thousands of photographs around me.

I reached out to the copper kandkaer jug to pour myself a glass of water. It stood on a newspaper. According to Father, our newspapers had turned into nothing less than 'mortuaries laid out on broadsheets'.

For me, they signalled the end of story-time with Bobeh. In the past months, she had become obsessed with newspapers, and instead of telling me folk tales like she used to in the past, she would spend time pointing at photographs that were printed in the dailies. She'd tug at the sleeve of my pheran and say, 'It is a mayhem! Karbala! *Vichi, vichi...*'

One night, Bobeh urged me to look at a photograph that had been printed in that day's papers – that of shoes and slippers scattered all over a street. In uneven pairs. As had become her habit, she inferred what she could from the frame aloud: 'People seemed to have fled. But why would they leave their chappals and shoes behind? That military voal looks alert. With his hands firmly placed on his loins, he is inspecting the road carefully. He is looking at ... something that I cannot see. Can you tell me what he is looking at so keenly? Where were all the people now, whose shoes were left behind? *Talay vuch...*'

I didn't respond to her, as I was drifting off to sleep, but my dream then turned out to be an extension of what Bobeh had narrated to me...

Part of the same tableau, I am standing on the other side of the road in a congregation of women. I can see myself, as if I am behind the frame as well as in it... There is a long streak of blood on my forehead, emerging from my hairline. I look shocked and angry. I feel scared looking at my own face.

I woke up and touched my face. Bobeh had left my side, but the newspaper lay there, with the photograph of the abandoned footwear.

The vivid dream caused by it had been too real and that gave me a headache. I wanted to stay away from the swathes of photographs published in the newspapers of unarmed, dead civilians. I wanted some physical distance from those pages, lest I dreamt of them again. But the more I wanted to peel myself away, the stronger their hold on me became.

Thankfully, the newspaper underneath the jug beside Bobeh's dead body was different. There was a sense of relief because it was not ours. I mean not from Kashmir. So, the chances of death smeared on it were minimal. I examined the coloured advertisement in one of the corners of the front page. It featured a woman next to a mattress with the words 'Guaranteed Comfort' floating above her head. Encouraged by the dreamy smile on the model's face, I opened the newspaper. I found an entire page filled with comics, a crossword puzzle, film releases, and half a page dedicated to weekly and monthly horoscope readings. My forecast said:

> You will feel the urge to expand your horizons, try new things, bigger and better things. You may have some luck with finances and possession, growing your net worth. You will be fortunate in romance as you appear mysterious to many!

HEART GOES BOOM-BOOM

'DO YOU REMEMBER WHICH CUPBOARD the kafan is in?'

'Yes. I'll accompany you upstairs. There are other things I need to take out of the cabinet too, or else we'll be scrambling during the morning rituals.'

Father left the room and Mother followed him. My aunt, Pophtaeth, and Ramzan Kaak were reciting the Quran next to Bobeh. No one sobbed loudly. The air was sombre as it is after the death of old people or those who die of natural causes, I thought, as I followed Mother and Father upstairs to their room.

Father unlatched the green door of a wooden cupboard in the antechamber adjacent to their room. Promptly, my eyes wandered to the large music system that they had bought from Saudi Arabia, where they, along with some other relatives, had gone for Hajj in the summer of 1988.

Other than the expected tabaruk – dates, Zam-Zam water, skullcap and tasbih – for relatives, acquaintances and neighbours, they'd bought many other gifts for friends and family members. Among the paraphernalia, crispy chocolate wafers were my favourite. The studded slippers were too gaudy for my liking, and, luckily, a size too small, so I never got to wear them.

For himself, Father had bought a large 'imported' music system. Father didn't particularly have varied taste in music. He was fond of Urdu ghazals by Mehdi Hassan, Kashmiri Sufi kalaam sung by Ghulam Hassan Sofi, like '*Afsoos duniya/ kaense na loab samsar saete*', and some soulful ones, such as '*Ruem gayam sheeshas begur govva baaneh myoan*' by Raj Begum and Naseem Akhtar. In those days, my favourite was a not-so-popular duet by Ghulam Hassan Sofi and Raj Begum: '*Valle tai vasiye dokh sokh masherith*'.

Before the big music system arrived at our house, we used to have a small stereo with two basic functions. It had a cavity to insert a tape into and an in-built radio. The new one had two spaces for tapes, an integrated, compact disc player at the top, and also a radio. Its edges were rounded and smooth, not boxy like the old one. It also had detachable speakers. All in all, it took up a fair bit of space. It stood out as one of the very few modern items in our traditional household.

Father rarely let anyone touch the music system. He was always around when he played it and after he was done, he stored it back carefully on the top shelf of the cupboard. He worried that if anything went wrong, the spare parts would be exorbitantly priced to be replaced.

Before my sister Hina got married, she'd take the music system out furtively and smuggle it into her room which was next to the antechamber. She'd get home from college late in the afternoon, but several hours ahead of Father's return from the shop. Hina would listen to her own tapes. Her playlist included songs by Pakistani pop artist Sajad Ali, 'Hawa Hawa' by Hassan Jahangir, and songs from Indian films like *Tridev*, *Qayamat Se Qayamat Tak* and *Mr X in Bombay*. Hina was very careful with the music system. She never forgot a tape inside and knew the exact angle at which Father had stored it in the cabinet.

Although, initially, she was apprehensive about letting me stick around during her clandestine musical afternoons, she came around after some months and let me into her surreal world. The only condition was that I made myself useful and did not disturb her. So, I'd pretend to prolong my homework and sit in her room with my books open. I was especially pleased when she played *Young Tarang* and 'Boom Boom' by the Pakistani sibling-duo Nazia and Zoheb Hassan. I liked Nazia's singing and her signature nasal twang so much that I harboured a secret wish to want to be a pop-singer when I grew up and not a doctor like Bobeh wanted me to become.

After Hina got married, Father moved the music system to the lower shelf of the cupboard. Not that he suspected Hina, but he was afraid of an imminent destruction of the system at the hands of angry troops at the time of a crackdown. A fear that was more than understandable, because a crackdown was nothing short of an out-of-body experience, no matter how many times one had been through it. Someone takes over your house without warning or permission, ransacks your bedroom, goes through all your things, turns your house upside-down and you're left either appeasing or pleading with them. The sound of boots on the wooden staircase would spark off a series of tremors in me. I would break into a sweat and panic so violently that I'd feel as if I could vomit my heart out. The reaction of troops upon seeing the music system was usually, *'Iss ke liye paisa kahaan se aata hai, saale madarchod aatankvaadiyo?'* That had instilled in Father a deep fear: he was convinced that it was just a matter of time before they'd vent their frustration on his prized possession. It was a surprise that they hadn't already.

Each time there was a crackdown, I muttered prayers hoping that no frustrated trooper tossed or flung the music system on to the floor even as they threw out utensils, clothes and books from the shelves, mercilessly, when 'searching' our kitchen and bedrooms.

A broken music system would be a loss to me than to anyone else. Father had more or less stopped listening to music since 1990. He was always on the alert for anything amiss and perhaps thought that the relaxation from music would come in between him and what was happening on the streets. For his news updates, he had a small transistor radio that he relied on.

When Hina got married, I stole one of her tapes, *Young Tarang* by Nazia and Zoheb Hassan. It included a mash-up of six of their best songs at the end of the album. Since school was hardly ever open in the three years between 1991 and 1993, quite frequently I'd carry the stereo to a forgotten storeroom at the back of our house, where Mother kept large trunks full of her trousseau and seasonal clothing. The dense air of the room was suffused with the migraine-inducing smell of naphthalene balls, but that never deterred me. During those secret afternoons, nothing could stop me from dancing to Nazia Hassan's '*Boom Boom*' and '*Disco Deewane*'. I'd pretend to hold a mic, swing my waist and hips, twirling while the air gathered under the crooks of my arms. I did that repeatedly until I felt sweaty, tired and out of breath inside that dingy room. Panting, I'd step outside to inspect if the corridor was empty so that I could safely place the music system back into its original place. Much later, even after my heart had calmed down, the rhythm of '*Boom, boom, dil bole boom, boom*' refused to disappear.

MAY I BECOME INVISIBLE, PLEASE?

MOTHER FOLLOWED FATHER AND ME into the antechamber after having performed wuzu. Water dripped from her face. Bobeh always advised against wiping or towel-drying our faces or arms after performing ablution.

'These are bad deeds and nazar falling off you in the form of drops. Let them.'

I didn't know how true it really was as I'd never heard anyone else say so, but it had become a habit of all our family members to pray with slightly damp hands, feet and faces.

Mother had the most luminous skin. Growing up, I had never seen her apply make-up. Once in a while, she'd indulge in applying henna to give her hair a sunset tinge. Hina, on the other hand, had developed an elaborate beauty regimen by the time she was eighteen. She and her friend Rifat regularly got their eyebrows threaded at a salon. They'd spend weekends at our house, making their own face mask with ground almonds and fresh cream. Hina refused to use store-bought shampoo and made her own concoction. She shopped from little lanes and by-lanes across Zaene Kadal for nutty roundels and dried herbs that went into her customized hair wash liquid. She would mix the carefully selected ingredients, boil them for hours until they turned into a liquid that looked like diluted cola with froth on top. She'd wait for it to cool before storing the mixture in large plastic containers. I was her helper, labelling the various bottles with sketch pens in my cursive writing. Watching Hina go about her beauty routine, I'd often wonder when I'd be old enough to start my own … but things turned out to be drastically different for me.

By the time I reached the age where the hair on my upper lip grew noticeably dark, salons had already been shut down. More than one hardliner faction, including Dukhtaran-e-Millat (Daughters of the Nation), which was headed by a woman, promulgated the Islamic codes for women by promoting a certain modest way of living. They denounced Western ways of dressing and ordered girls and women to cover their heads with scarves.

In school, a new dress code was announced when we started eighth standard. We were presented with a choice – to either wear skirts for another year or switch to white shalwar-kameez paired with a coloured sash. Some of us had been gearing up to keep wearing skirts by starting to shave our legs and rolling our socks to our ankles, like our seniors. Just before the school day was over and the gates opened, we'd make a quick trip to the washroom. When we emerged, we flaunted high ponies and lowered socks. It made us feel grown up; somewhat feminine, somewhat modern. Even though it was an all-girls school, we'd get into serious trouble if we were caught. The punishment could range from a small monetary fine, a note to our parents from the vice principal, to being publicly shamed at the morning assembly. We dreaded all of these, but they were nothing compared to the price Nuzhat paid for not adhering to the newly announced dress codes by the moral factions.

Nuzhat, a lanky, tomboyish teenager, was one of my classmates. She lived in Dalgate. She and her mother were walking near Nehru Park, one of the busiest and equally militarized areas of the city, when two boys riding a scooter threw acid on her.

Shabnam, her neighbour, another classmate of ours, broke the news to us in school. 'Nuzhat was wearing jeans. Her head was uncovered at the time of the attack,' said a newly hijab-clad Shabnam.

Three weeks later, Nuzhat resumed school. She became an object of warning for us. We took turns to see her injuries. She'd pull the sleeve of her white school uniform to bare a contrasting brown scar on her left shoulder, right where her collar bone ended. When she was asked 'Did it hurt?' or 'Are you scared?' or 'Show us the scar!', she answered with just one sentence, as if she'd crammed her emotions in it, 'Can you imagine, I turned my face away!'

Eventually, things eased out. The enforcement of new codes didn't last too long. The outfits that demanded the new, 'more Islamic' ways of living, lost relevance. Salons started operating again, although secretly, without the sign boards. Many women who worked at salons before, started door-to-door beauty services and soon got enough work through word of mouth. By then, I had practised threading my upper lip one full winter and didn't need to visit a beautician to do the task. Some of my female relatives, who lived in the vicinity, would visit me to get their upper lips and eyebrows threaded because they thought it was safer to get it done from someone they knew than at a salon. One of them became so fond of me that she was rather keen on getting me married to her only son. Perhaps, she was of the notion that my threading skills would be a matter of lifelong convenience for her!

Some girls and women, who had grown accustomed to wearing headscarves, continued to do so. I too covered my hair in sporadic spurts because I had actively started pulling my hair out since that fateful day in 1989 when I had been presumed to be dead. With a scarf wrapped around my head, I could easily hide my bald patches. I trimmed my own hair to keep it looking fluffy under the scarf.

With troopers stationed everywhere, walking on the streets made me feel uneasy. It felt like I was inviting their lecherous gaze. Like many others in the neighbourhood, I had cut down on going out, but there were trips that were unavoidable: to school, for tuitions, to the tailor. To an extent, the scarf made me feel protected, and yet, that feeling of unease never quite left me completely. And so, I began to ignore caring for my skin.

I thought maybe if I looked ugly and less pleasant, the men would not look at me and I'd be safe. I wouldn't wash my face for days. I didn't want to look attractive in any way, at all, lest it invited undue attention and that indescribable guilt. I wanted to somehow become invisible.

Suddenly during those months, an old, black-and-white film that I had seen on TV as a young girl made sense to me. It was the story of a young woman of marriageable age, who spent most of her time being devoted to a deity. As expected of any girl her age, she was under a lot of family pressure to get married. But she did not want that for herself; she wanted to commit herself to spirituality. In her struggle to fight her family, and the society at large, she sought the intervention of gods. She had a simple wish: to lose her youthful appearance. Her wish was granted. In a second, she lost her youthful looks. Wrinkly skin and grey hair appeared; she developed a visible hunchback too. Thereafter, no one came in her way and she could live her life on her own terms. I, too, desperately wished that I could vanish, escape everyone's gaze, and not attract any unwanted attention. Not be thrown acid at like Nuzhat, not to be stared at by the troops.

THE COUNTRY WITH A BURNT POST OFFICE

MOTHER COLLECTED THE SHROUD, A green cloth embroidered with Quranic verses, a box of incense sticks, and a packed bar of soap that would be needed the next day for burial.

'Can you help me put these back in the cupboard?' She asked me to fold the chadors and some unstitched pieces of cloth that she'd taken out of various bags.

It was common practice for Father to bring reams of fabric from the shop for Mother. However, she didn't always get all of them stitched. Instead, she kept some aside or gave away some as gifts to relatives. That cupboard was her treasure trove.

She and Father rushed downstairs.

I sat alone in the antechamber of their bedroom, folding the pieces of fabric and arranging them on the almirah shelves. The pieces I was trying to fold were puffed up. I had to refold them, match the original creases, put them into bags, and then readjust the bags so the shelves wouldn't spill over. It made my task more time-consuming and my arms felt fatigued. While arranging the cloth and bags, I stumbled upon a soft leather bag full of LPs, old Urdu magazines, and an old blazer which was part of my school uniform at some point. I looked at the LP covers, and then, out of curiosity, checked the pockets of the green blazer. I was surprised to find an old letter that I had written to Vaseem in 1993. I hadn't expected that unsent love letter to spring out from an unlikely corner of the house…

Most break-ups are painful. Some are acrimonious. Mine was neither. I lost my first love to a burnt post-office. It was a romance that was cut short by fire. A romance that had blossomed on the balcony of Baji, my maternal aunt, and ended up in smoke.

Three years after Tehreek began, I was to finally graduate from high school. The annual exams at the end of 1992 worried Mother more than me. As soon as the schedule of the pre-boards was out, Mother solemnly declared the weeks to follow to be the 'most crucial'. She decided to send me to her sister Razia's house in Raj Bagh. I fondly called that aunt of mine, Baji.

Baji lived near my school, and that would give me more time to revise and less time to be anxious about the commute. I was expected to return home after the final paper, which would be held in two weeks' time.

Baji's large house was tucked away in a small and quiet neighbourhood, far away from the madness of the city. Though calm prevailed outside in their neighbourhood, their joint family ensured that there was none inside the house. With about twelve family members, their house was always noisy and full of pleasant distractions. The men – her sons, husband, brother-in-law and his son – owned two shops and a small motel near the restive Maisuma Bazar. Since the area was under constant siege – because that is where Yasin Malik, one of the four founders of JKLF (Jammu and Kashmir Liberation Front), lived – they usually stayed home.

With a tight exam schedule, and hardly a day in between papers, I had no luxury to dawdle. During the daytime, as there was rarely a quiet moment indoors, I turned the balcony outside Baji's bedroom into my study. The balcony overlooked her manicured rose garden. Weeping willows lined the tranquil alleyway. It made a pleasing canopy that kept the afternoon sun at bay. The breeze rustled the leaves, creating a soothing and understated symphony that made it more conducive to napping than studying.

Baji would join me for nun chai at four o'clock on the balcony. One such afternoon, she walked in with the tea, and the date sheet that had been published in a newspaper was on the tray too. The sight of newspaper made me nervous.

'It's so peaceful here. We can't even imagine this calm in the tense downtown of ours. It used to be one of the busiest streets, but it's so scary now. Something or the other keeps happening there. You can't study in peace anymore. I miss sitting on the windowsill with Bobeh. We rarely get to open the windows. I wish our home was as cocooned as yours,' I said.

Baji raised both her eyebrows, as if in disbelief. A sudden fear came over her face. '*Kyah tchakh vanaan*? Don't you remember most of the dead on Gaw Kadal were from here? From around this area? Right there across the bund is where most of them lived: in Mahjoor Nagar, Radio Colony, Ikhraaj pur...' She then stared at the staircase leading to the bund.

Our tea got cold. I didn't know what to say to my aunt who had not only gone silent but also had a faraway look in her eyes. Was she still thinking about the firing at Gaw Kadal in 1990? I picked up the newspaper. Both her silence and daze were broken by a greeting. She was responding to Vaseem, her sister-in-law's son, who lived nearby.

Vaseem was older than me by four years. I had seen him cycle past their house sometimes. He'd smile at me. I noticed that he didn't have an aquiline nose or bony features like the rest of us. His cheeks had somehow still retained their redness. He looked more Ladakhi than Kashmiri, I thought. Same, nonetheless.

On the day of my second exam, I was walking back from school when I spotted a racer bike approaching me. It was him. He braked swiftly and boldly struck up a conversation with me. Most of the boys I had known then would usually hatch a complicated plan with their friends if they wanted to talk to a girl. It felt mildly awkward speaking to a known stranger. He was very confident. I didn't resist. I noticed that he had a thin line of very fine lashes, which were only visible when his smile crinkled his eyes.

'Salaam ... Aren't you Baji's niece from Zaene Kadal?'

'Yes.'

'I am Vaseem. Qazi sa'ab's son. I am studying outside Kashmir. How was your paper today?'

'I think it went off well. Thanks.'

'When is your next paper?'

'Day after. Okay, Baji must be waiting. Bye.'

'Bye.'

As I walked away, he whispered, 'I think your eyes are beautiful.'

I didn't respond, but I believe it was then that I fell in love with him.

As my exams neared their end, the frequency of Vaseem riding past Baji's house increased. And of course, our exchanging glances didn't escape the eyes of Baji's curious neighbours. But as luck would have it, I left for home right after my exams, and soon after, Vaseem left for his college in Bangalore. Thankfully, there was no full-fledged neighbourhood gossip.

After the exams, we returned to school for the last few months. One afternoon, as I was about to board the school bus for home, the security guard at the gate came running towards the bus. I panicked thinking that he had probably come bearing some bad news. Should I duck in case he heard gunshots that we may have missed? Should we run to seek refuge in the library because the search operations had begun? I stood frozen as these scenarios rushed through my head and couldn't move while he rushed towards me, panting.

'Your relative is here. He has an urgent packet for you.'

Relative? Who? Perplexed, I tried to recognize the unexpected and unannounced relation of mine from a distance. Much to my surprise, I found out it was Farooq Bhaiya. I felt a strange knot in my belly.

Farooq Bhaiya was a friend of one of Baji's sons. He was also friends with Vaseem and his elder brother. My heart sank at the anticipation of receiving news about Vaseem. But Farooq Bhaiya had brought a letter. I received it with slight hesitation but was eager to know its contents. I did not open it immediately. I held on to the letter all through the bus ride, and after reaching home, sneaked into the bathroom before Bobeh could feed me lunch. My stomach churned as I tore the envelope open. I felt a warm sensation spread all over me as I read the first few lines and realized that there was no bad news. Stuck on the letter, there were cute Archies' stickers, which, if it were bad news, wouldn't have been there. Phew! Thereafter, I read the letter a few times a day for several days. Each time, I felt the same way.

Vaseem had found a way to reach me while he was away, but for me the challenge was to send replies. I could keep one ready when he sent a missive. but I wanted to find an alternate way. Even though the big building of the General Post Office was visible from our school, across river Jhelum, it was impossible to leave school to go there, post a letter and come back in time to catch the school bus. There were serious restrictions over leaving school before time. I thought through several solutions before bribing Nadia, a friend of mine, who lived close to the post office. I'd give her colourful gel stickers that we used to embellish our notebooks with. I begged her to drop the envelope at the counter inside as I had little faith in the defunct, little, red box outside our school. I'd never seen anyone pick mail from it or drop any into it.

Eventually, a routine was set. Vaseem and I wrote to each other nearly for a year. We developed a keen friendship through letters but within a few weeks, the conversations began to feel more intimate. We quoted poems and sent each other birthday cards. He mentioned short trips he would take with his friends around his college while I wrote about my studies and sleeplessness. He confessed to missing me and expressed that there were times when he wished he didn't have to leave home to find a life elsewhere. I began to envision our relationship blossoming into the distant but definitive reality of marriage and children.

However, staying in touch was proving to be a challenge. The post was largely undependable and phone lines were frequently dead. One of his letters reached me twenty-two days after he had posted it, almost a week after his arrival at home for his short vacation around the holidays in March. Luckily, it was the time for unit tests, and I succeeded in convincing Mother that I needed to stay at Baji's house and study.

I wanted to welcome Vaseem with a present. But with my meagre pocket money, a gift other than a cheap soft toy was ruled out. Would he even like it? I decided on flowers instead. If I were to pluck some red poppy from Baji's garden, she'd come to know. I was sure that she counted her flowers. So, I gathered some hollyhocks and irises which grew over the walls of her neighbour's garden. I made a bouquet and sent it to Vaseem through my youngest cousin, Raafi. I had to bribe him with twenty rupees to maintain secrecy.

I expected Vaseem to 'accidentally' run into me on the way to or from school. But we couldn't meet. A curfew was imposed in the city the day after I arrived at Baji's place. A number of people had come out on to the streets to commemorate the civilian killings in Tengpur. Vaseem spent a few days under curfew at home and had to leave without seeing me. I was annoyed. Angry, even. Fucking curfews! An unending cycle of curfews! Why couldn't we protest? Aren't people allowed to mourn when their loved ones die? Must more people get killed while mourning?

Vaseem and I continued to write to each other for a few more months until that dreamy world of letters between us also ended up in smoke. One night, a fire broke out in the main post office building, burning with it the only means of our communication. There was no rush to restore or repair it. That wasn't surprising, because living in a conflict zone had taught us that the broken stayed broken for a long time. The post office became functional after over a year, but we didn't resume writing.

I had tucked away all of Vaseem's letters in the storeroom with a stack of old newspapers and magazines. Somehow, one incomplete letter was left behind in the uniform blazer.

Salaam V

'Gates of memory never close, how much I miss you nobody knows'

Remember, you had written to me about how you imagine me on these streets? I don't know what you imagine … It's not the same anymore. The bustle created at the shops of gold and coppersmiths, the dancing dresses as you'd call the flowy, shimmering, sequined cloth hanging from shops are gone.

It used to be so lively here as you might remember when you visited Khankah-i-Maula. Every evening was like a celebration. Now that bustle is replaced by sadness. People look worrisome. Nobody speaks loudly like we used to. Is curfew controlling our vocal cords too? The only loud sound we hear is shopkeepers rolling their shutters down when the 'relaxation' is over. There is hush on the streets and even a slight sound brings with it an echo of fear.

There is rush at the time of announcement that declares the thirty-five-minute-long relaxation in the curfew in the evenings. Can you imagine? Half an hour out of twenty-four hours is not enough. Streets are full of people out to buy basics. Not everyone is lucky enough to get all the things that they need. You know, Mother sent Ramzan Kaak to buy toothpaste for two days in a row. He came back and said, 'There were more urgent things that people needed to buy for their children.' But on the third day, Mother told him strictly that he must push his way inside the shop or else we will never get what we need. Her fear was the shopkeeper might soon run out of basic hygiene items.

Stationery shops rarely open anymore. My notebooks are half-filled, some of which I use now to write these letters to you. I am sorry, I am out of letter-pads. I do not know when we will get them again. I also miss sketching. I draw and make patterns on the borders of old newspapers. The patterns that brides have on their hennaed hands. I make those on the newspapers. Newspapers make everyone so sad. Especially Bobeh. Sheets full of endless, countless funerals. Everyone has been inside their homes for weeks now. What becomes of homes that have their doors bolted, windows tightly shut, and curtains drawn during the daytime with the families they house inside them desolate? Should we not call them prisons? We should!

I don't know when I will post these letters to you. I might have to hand these over when you are back and if we meet when you are home. I'll tell you about the rest when we meet, if we meet. What if they impose curfew again when you are home? Will we meet? I hate curfews. I want to pick the petals of a flower. It's so sad that we do not have a garden like yours or Baji's. I could pick petals and play that stupid game they show in films – he loves me, he loves me not. I could change that to – will they impose curfew: Maybe, Maybe not.

Dec 1992

PERIOD PANGS AND A STRAY BULLET

IT IS FASCINATING HOW FAST people adapt to their new circumstances. It's as if the old ones never existed. It must have felt so different to move about the house at midnight without feeling extreme fear. But the carefree circumstances of the time before 1989 had turned into ghosts. After 1989, it didn't feel like we lived in the same house, especially at night. Father had all the bright lights replaced with zero-watt bulbs, which made the passages visible, hence walkable. There were nights when

I didn't dare take a trip to the toilet, especially when I was on my period.

On ordinary, sleepless nights, I'd wait in bed in anticipation of the day to break and catch some sleep towards dawn. On unpredictable nights of the month, when muscle spasms and menstrual cramps were the only certainty, getting through was an ordeal, both physical and emotional. I wasn't one of those lucky girls whose periods came and went like nothing had happened. My cramps usually started before the period and lasted for days. Sometimes, even three anti-spasmodic tablets would not subside the pain. Managing by distracting myself during the day was still bearable, but at night, it meant enduring crippling pain and discomfort, silently. I kept myself well-prepared and made sure to keep essential things handy.

Barkat: A glass of water poured in an intricately carved, tall, copper glass

Chhirkatt: A rectangular plastic packet

Myakatt: Two painkillers

Haput: A small, black polythene bag

Ponz: An extra pair of panties

It was a peculiar way of counting that I had learnt from Ramzan Kaak. It made no sense, but the first three words rhymed well and the two latter ones were just amusing.

Barkat, Chhirkatt, Myakatt, Haput, Ponz

(Blessings, Goat, Lamb, Bear, Monkey)

After he was done assisting Father at the shop, Ramzan Kaak would return home with at least five different kinds of sweetmeats and candies for me. These included dried dates, slivers of dried coconut, shereen (tiny sugar balls), sangtar methai (orange-flavoured candy) and besrakh (a slice of dried pastry). I'd stretch out my small, cupped palms. He'd place kyencza in them, one by one. I grew older but didn't outgrow the habit of counting five items his way especially during that time of the month.

During the day, I usually placed a cinnamon stick in my mouth to rid myself of nausea caused by the period. But the nights were full of agony. The spasms routinely started after midnight as soon as the effect of the post-dinner tablet would wear off. I'd pop another tablet but for that to take effect meant suffering excruciating pain for another hour or so. Tossing and turning, turning and tossing, I would curl up into a foetal position, pushing the knees deep into my stomach to alleviate the pain. It must have looked like some mysterious monthly dance routine in the dark.

Once, I had run out of the anti-spasmodic medicine. The thought of fetching some paracetamol from the living room, or to get a stick of cinnamon from the kitchen at night, was unthinkable! The curfew had its own way of slipping indoors. It was impossible to move about anywhere in the house without causing alarm. All the staircases inside the house were made of wood. Even tiptoeing on those made them creak. Who knew which of those noises would travel outside and alert the troops to barge inside the house? Sounds could attract a volley of bullets fired in your direction, unwarranted. It was a thought that kept me stuck to my mattress, writhing in pain.

Who had the courage to take the stairs to the kitchen which was just a floor below the bedrooms? It was not an insurmountable distance to cover during the day but seemed far away during those unending nights. Most of the houses in the old city didn't have toilets attached to the bedrooms. They were usually connected to the house through a passage. It meant passing through a circuitous corridor, opening, shutting, bolting and unbolting several wooden doors. No matter how careful one was or how well lubricated the hinges were, the wooden structures in the old part of the city let out a shrill noise on being opened and emitted a hollow thud when they were shut.

It hadn't been long since an asthmatic and unassuming neighbour, the grandmother of a friend, paid a heavy price for causing a stir at night. One night, she experienced a shortness of breath and decided to let in some fresh air. As she flung one of her bedroom windows open, the wooden planks jostling against each other made some noise. Just then, a bullet flew in from nowhere and hit the seventy-five-year-old woman, killing her instantly. Instead of catching fresh air to ease her laboured breathing, her heart was neatly pierced. Such bad luck for the poor woman to come in the way of a stray bullet, I thought, when we learnt about the incident the next day.

During a period, on at least two consecutive nights every month, the pain had to be borne silently without attempting to find ways to alleviate it. I'd have rather continued to lie quietly, cry, and let my hair soak up the tears through the night, than attract dangers for the family.

DJINN AND JAHANAM

IT WAS PAST MIDNIGHT. I wanted to pray for Bobeh, but couldn't. Despite Mother's repeated instructions to do so, I resisted. My eyes were heavy from loss, from fatigue. I looked at the rectangular tin box in which Bobeh kept her medicines. It lay next to her body. I knew it also had my medication that could help me fall asleep and also calm me down. I had those small pills sometimes, as a doctor had advised me. I took them with great caution. I was scared that I'd end up like Abida's mother. Her being depended on them.

When I was much younger, around seven or eight years old, I would be petrified by a story told by my friend and a distant cousin, Abida. She and I were the same age. We went to the same school, took the same school bus. She didn't live very far from our house. Sometimes, I'd stay over at her place. When we'd get ready to go to bed, she'd tell me the same story.

'There are two cats that come to life at night. They control my movements, my sleep, my words. They have full control over me,' she'd say in a grave, heavy tone. To make it more frightening, she'd add, 'They sleep under the bed, only I can see them. They are not visible to anyone else, not even my parents, not even Mumma. Go, check for yourself if you don't believe me. You won't see anything. They trouble the person who is rude to me, including my Mumma.' I was too scared, and never dared to look under the bed and call her bluff.

Abida was a wiry and petite girl. Her distinguishing feature was her light-coloured eyes. When she'd tell me the scary-cat story, her glassy pair of eyes appeared bigger and brighter. I think I gave the cat story more importance and credence because of her mother, Jaaji. Jaaji was known to have tasruf and be under the spell of a spirit that manifested itself through her from time to time. A couple of times, she had threatened violence against her family but had never harmed anyone. She had run after her husband with a box of matches to set him on fire though.

Her two children, Abida and her younger, sister, Sabia, were kept away from Jaaji during such times, but the rest of the relatives who had seen her during or soon after an episode, said that she would change beyond recognition. Her voice became coarse, her light eyes turned vacuous and her movements jerky. During the 'spells', Jaaji would apparently become physically stronger. Her scaredy-mouse of a husband didn't dare to go near her. Her petite frame had to be overpowered either with help from the males in the house or by a priest-cum-exorcist.

'*Neyrkha kinih kadath*? Will you leave, or shall I drive you out?' the priest was heard threatening the ghost in the dimly lit room where he performed exorcism rituals. Their conversations were somewhat audible to the family members outside the room. They could hear Jaaji's voice transform into a rough, adult male voice.

During her outbursts, the spirit that possessed Jaaji demanded various things. One time, it had asked that three whole chickens be fed to it within fifteen minutes. It had threatened to poison the family meals if the demand wasn't met. There was one other demand that was so peculiar that it became the stuff of legends. The spirit had frightened the entire family by telling them that it would reside in Jaaji's body forever and had additionally sworn to raze the entire house down.

'*Baanavkha astaan nebrikani kinih na?*' it had asked. 'Will you make a shrine for me or not?' That was the big ask. A small shrine had to be constructed near the main market of Boher Kadal. The spirit, through Jaaji, had drafted the precise blueprint of the shrine in seven minutes flat and specified the exact location.

Under dire circumstances, a shrine was constructed overnight. It is said that right after the work on the shrine was completed, on that very day, the poltergeist had fled Jaaji's body. It didn't return for a long, long while.

Unfortunately, the incident had also made a hero out of the priest on whom Abida's family had increasingly become dependent not only to cure Jaaji, but also to extract the messages from spirits in general. Since the djinn had obeyed the man, he was considered irreplaceable.

After 1989, as curfews and instances of round-the-clock cross-firing increased in frequency, it became difficult for their family to fetch the priest from his village. It'd take half a day to call on him and another half to bring him to the city. Every time Abida's mother had an episode, before the news could reach the relatives who could come to her rescue and by the time the priest arrived and began his exorcism rituals, the loud banging of the doors and her screams would rouse the neighbours.

Fearing that her episodes, which would last anything from an hour to days, might attract undue attention from the troops stationed on the streets and in the gullies, Jaaji had to be hushed. There was no other way! Finally, her in-laws and parents collectively decided to take her to a doctor. Though the topic had been a bone of contention between the two families, her behavioural disorder eventually brought them closer. Jaaji's in-laws had always accused her parents of withholding crucial information about the bride's mental health before her marriage. Her parents claimed and maintained that Jaaji had never exhibited such behaviour before the wedding. While both the families were bitter over this, hurling blame at each other, they had never thought of consulting a psychiatrist until they realized the danger her episodes was putting them in, in relation to the troops.

After being prescribed pills by the psychiatrist, Jaaji's episodes reduced. But what also went away with that was her vitality and her beauty. As she became more dependent on her medication, she could barely digest her food and vomited often. She was unable to look after her children and carry out her household duties, which her mother-in-law, at the age of seventy, now had to take care of.

Mother, who had visited her once, came back sadder. '*Bichaari, Djinn draas, jahanam aas.* Poor thing, she may have been exorcized for good, but she has turned into a living corpse,' she told Bobeh. Mother's eyes moistened as she described Jaaji. 'She is crippled. Her brown curls look like burnt hay on top of her head. She used to look like an empress with her high cheekbones, but now those bones make her look like an exhumed corpse, *qabri manz kedmicz*. Her lips rarely ever needed lip-stain but today, they looked chapped and ashen. Seeing her, I was in two minds. Was it really Jaaji sitting on the mattress or had the ghost decided to permanently live in her body? Her children do not go near her. I don't know if they can even tell that that's their mother.'

By dint of her having a mother who was the medium between this world and the occult, most of Abida's friends, including me, treated her with some degree of fear and curiosity. We were careful not to sit too close to her lest she too possessed supernatural powers like Jaaji. Abida, in the meanwhile, relied more and more on the imaginary cats; she brought them up in every conversation. Then, she became elusive.

But then it was not just Jaaji and Abida alone. More faces resembling Jaaji's started appearing in the streets, and the number of patients outside the psychiatrist clinics increased rapidly. Three years later, a reflection of Jaaji appeared in my mirror when I too was prescribed sedatives and SSRI medications.

In 1993, just before I turned seventeen, I showed symptoms of heightened anxiety. I'd get palpitations, sleeplessness, and was inexplicably restless. I often contemplated various means by which to commit suicide. For weeks, I wouldn't speak more than a few words a day. I preferred to stay inside a dimly lit room during the day. I detested sunlight. Anything that the sun touched seemed torched to me. If a ray managed to pass through the thick curtains, that remained drawn throughout the day – it felt like it was going to consume the whole room, including me. Doctors diagnosed the condition as Post Traumatic Stress Disorder or PTSD, like they did for everyone else. Mir, a friend of mine, once joked that the acronym's expansion needed a revision in Kashmir. It should have stood for Perennially Traumatic Stress Disorder, he said.

EARLY HOURS

ROLL CALL

IN HER LATE TEENS, FATHER'S youngest sister, Nelofar, had a dream. Thereafter, she decided – for a brief period, though – to never marry and devote her entire life to spirituality. Nelofar recounted her dream only to Bobeh. Both then narrated it to Noori sa'ab, the revered priest at the nearby shrine of the sufi saint, Sheikh Yaqoob Sarfi. Noori sa'ab was among the last of the elders to wear a huge, white turban. With his long and flowy white beard and droopy eyes, he exuded a saintly aura to match his demeanour. Other than naming the children of his devotees, he was also the locality's trusted interpreter of dreams. In Islam, dreams are accorded great importance, as a lot of messages in the Quran were revealed through dreams. In our home, dreams weren't ignored either. They were discussed, interpretations were tried by elders, and if further demystification was needed, Noori sa'ab's consultation was sought. He'd ruminate over the dream for a couple of days before revealing its cryptic message. His first advice used to be either donating alms to the poor or feeding them. Noori sa'ab would sometimes say, '*Hoonis traevzi tczoat*', suggesting that feeding stray dogs could ward off the evil that the dream may have revealed upon sober and deeper reflection.

I had a dream. I had just turned fourteen and this recurring dream was bothering me a lot. In the dream, the names of the students from my class and the ones of our teachers were all mixed up. Although it was funny at first, I began to wonder if I should speak about it to someone wiser for an interpretation. I should ask Bobeh before it is too late, I thought. I didn't end up asking anyone, though, but noted down the names that appeared in my dream in the hope that the writing would reveal something.

    Iffat Maqbool (teacher) – *present*
    Jyoti Raina (teacher) – *absent*
    Renuka Bazaz (student) – *absent*
    Gopi Nath Kaul (teacher) – *absent*
    Farah Bashir (student) – *present*
    Sir Bali (teacher) – *present*
    Maria Mendonza (student) – *present*
    Sister Ida (teacher) – *present*
    Sister Bonnyventure (teacher) – *present*

Pujinder Kaur (student) – *present*
Asiya Hassan (student) – *present*
Sunita Malhotra (teacher) – *present*
Yogita Bali (teacher) – *present*
Mrs Suri (teacher) – *present*
Sister Martha (teacher) – *present*
Sadaf Butt (student) – *present*
Sumera Shah (student) – *absent*
Laxmisree Kaul (student) – *absent*

The order of absentees wasn't consistent throughout. Sometimes, the dream presented reality as it were. Sumera Shah was constantly absent, which was a fact in real life. Her family, like many other rich families, had businesses outside the valley, where they would usually spend the winter months. But this time around, they did not return home after the vacation. Sumera only spent exam weeks with us. Her grades suffered. 'It's difficult to study by oneself. The syllabus is different there. And I don't have any friends! I want to come back,' she told us during one of her 'exam trips'. But from overheard adult conversations, we knew they weren't going to be back anytime soon. Theirs was one of the well-off families that were routinely targeted by the militants for donations of large sums of money. So, they preferred staying away and visited home only when necessary.

Soon after, the dream mix-up ceased to be amusing and it presented a constantly niggling question. Why was it that the ones 'present' included only my Sikh and Christian friends and teachers, but hardly any of the Pandits? At that point, I didn't dare ask Bobeh about the dream because I thought the odd mention of Laxmisree Kaul would upset her.

As it was, after the winter of 1990, when we could no longer see the light in Laxmisree's room across the alley, Bobeh would heave long sighs, which in turn aggravated her wheezing. She often stared at the window of Laxmisree's room.

Bobeh was very fond of Laxmisree and always spoke highly of her. 'She's such a hard worker! For her, her studies are no less than ibadat. She's always up before I wake up for Tahhjudd. No matter how busy she is, she never forgets to say adab arz to me.' She always furrowed her right eyebrow as she commented on her ideal neighbour. Laxmisree was studying medicine. It was possible for Bobeh to know her exact study hours because our houses were situated next to each other. The back of their house faced the left side of ours. Laxmisree's room and the room where Bobeh used to pray were separated by a narrow koche, a slit of a space.

Before the Kauls left in 1990, whenever there was a celebratory function to be held at Laxmisree's house, the two houses were connected by a wooden plank, pilav, merging them into one. The last time that happened was in September 1988, when Laxmisree's elder sister's son, Kartik, was born. A feast was thrown to celebrate his birth across both the houses. I'd imagined two more feasts that would have connected the households. One would have been when Laxmisree completed her MBBS and I, mine.

'*Jildich doctor baenzi*. Become a dermatologist,' Bobeh often advised me. I doubt if she had ever had the need to visit one, but I guessed that she couldn't bear the idea of me being on call during the nights. Often, when I'd fall asleep without eating dinner, she'd feed me in my sleep. She recognized the hard work that I'd need to put in were I to study medicine, yet she was relieved at the idea that that would end in a few years. Bobeh had realized that the chances of a skin specialist being required during late night emergencies at the hospital were next to nil. Or perhaps, Laxmisree had told her so from across the alley during their conversations.

But what remained unsaid between the two of them was the terror Laxmisree must have felt when her college senior Dr Rubaiya Sayeed was kidnapped by militants as she was coming out of Lal Ded Hospital, where she worked as an intern. The militants, who were released in exchange of her, near Father's shop in Boher Kadal, received celebratory gunfire. People came out on the streets like it was the eve of Eid. At night, they blared anti-India, pro-resistance slogans from the loud speakers of the mosques. I hoped to catch Laxmisree's eye one day and ask her if she knew Dr Rubaiya Sayeed well, or if she knew anyone who had seen the militants take her hostage. But the truth was that I was too terrified myself to ask such questions. In any case, none of us saw Laxmisree or her mother, whom we fondly called Kaakyen, appear on the windows anymore. It was less than a month after that incident that the lights of their house went off permanently.

At the onset of winter, it was a common practice to shut windows tightly until the air turned warmer in spring. Laxmisree and Bobeh still opened their respective ones, from time to time, even amid the harsh cold. One did so to let fresh air in for studying, and the other did so to fight bouts of breathlessness caused by asthma. They'd give each other quiet company. But in that winter of 1990, all the windows turned into walls.

After the name mix-up in the dream, I noticed more Sikhs around me: whether it was the Sikh boys when they'd be drying their hair on the porches of their homes, and we would so admire their hair, or Dr Sethi, the pediatrician, whose clinic I would visit with my sister Hina whenever my nephew Moosa needed medical attention. In fact, the head carpenter who renovated parts of our home before my sister's wedding was Kirpal Singh, or Sardarji (as Bobeh liked to call him). When I wanted to get my nose pierced, for instance, and Hina suggested that I get it done by someone at a Sikh jeweller's shop, it didn't strike me as something odd. She had hers pieced by a neighbourhood Muslim jeweller and it had taken weeks for her nose to heal before she could wear the tiny monga pin that Bobeh had gifted her.

'Get your nose pierced at Tara Singh Jewellers,' she suggested. 'You can go to any of their shops at Hari Singh High Street. My friend Rifat got hers done from there much after I did but she got to wear her chinar-shaped silver nose-pin much before I got to wear mine.' She was right. The technicians at Tara Jewellers were skilled indeed. My thick nostril didn't feel much pain or discomfort, and it healed within a week.

At school, there were many Sikh teachers and none of them were absent in life or in the dream. There was Mrs Suri (Chemistry), Mrs Jamwal (English), Mrs Iqbal (Maths), Mrs Chand (English), Ms Bali (Maths), and the loveliest Mrs Sunita Singh, who taught us grooming and presentation skills, and whose charm inspired generations of students. Then, of course, there was Mr Bali, the sports teacher. He always ensured that he was the last to leave the school premises. He didn't step out until all of us had safely left for the day, especially if the 'situation was tense' anywhere in the city.

PASIKDAR: THE BENIGN SPIRIT

'AYAT-AL-KURSI WILL PROTECT YOU FROM all evil. You must always recite it before going to bed' – used to be Bobeh's routine advice to my sister and me.

I awoke from my nap to a loud thud outside our living room. The sound caused a momentary hollowing out of my throat, as if I'd lost the ability to breathe or speak. My heart felt like it was about to leap out of my chest. Involuntarily, I mumbled Ayat-ul-Kursi. In the beginning of the 1990s, when I wasn't sure of what was happening in the neighbourhood, those words had become my amulet. Most often, none of us could muster the courage to peep out of the windows and see what the sounds were about. We'd stay put in our respective spots and I would recite Ayat-al-Kursi.

Fear used to be of a different kind before 1990. In the summer of 1988, Father's aunt Fatima was visiting us from her village Parnewa near Budgam. My sister Hina and I shared our bedroom with her. Deep into the dead of the night, both Hina and I were awakened by some noises: of things being moved and perhaps paper being crumpled. We stiffened like corpses.

Bobeh's advice came in handy, as always. I recited the verses. She had also told us about every house being guarded by a usually benign spirit called Pasikdar, who is averse to naapaeki – impurity of any kind – and punishes the impure.

'Pasikdar loves cleanliness,' she'd often tell us. 'He never troubles the members of a family who perform ablution before sleeping, and those who keep their bedding and clothes clean. In fact, every night, he guards the people who recite Ayat-al-Kursi. But if you are unclean, he will crush your chest with the weight of his foot, and you won't be able to move. *Brokus kornam kaanyen raatas.*' Sometimes, Bobeh narrated painful experiences about being trampled upon by Pasikdar which made it a scarier possibility than just an innocuous inculcation of a good habit. If he could hurt her, he wouldn't spare us.

That night after midnight, as Hina and I awoke to the sound of crumpling of paper, petrified, reciting Ayat-al-Kursi, we kept wondering if we were going to be let off with a warning or if a larger punishment lay in store for us. Pasikdar was known to create supernatural noises as a kind of 'notice' for mortals before inflicting a proper punishment on them. We clutched each other's hands tightly, wondering which one of us was wearing unclean clothes and who had provoked the wrath of the spirit. But it seemed like both of us deserved punishment. I had shut my eyes firmly and would open them for a brief second only to shut them again.

Suddenly, a voice asked us, '*Sangtar khash gaczvai?*'

It couldn't have been Pasikdar. He wasn't known to indulge in dialogue.

Turned out it wasn't him trying to punish us, but Father's aunt who had been gorging on an orange. As per her old habit to snack at odd hours, it was she who was eating without the dentures on. The squishy noises made by her eating made the atmosphere ghostly and frightening. Oblivious to our misery, she had asked us if we too had woken up feeling hungry and offered us her snack. 'Would you like an orange?' she asked again.

Much braver than me, Hina spoke up: '*Taethi, tczi tchakhai hushaar*? Aunt, are you awake?

'*Phreth koruth mye*! You scared me!' Hina said and sighed.

'Me too,' I added quickly. 'I was clutching your hand so hard.'

'*Kyah goam, kyah goam*! You girls are too funny, scared of an orange,' she chided us while continuing to eat and chuckle. 'How can you be afraid of someone eating an orange?' The chuckling continued.

Hina and I were relieved. We recounted the incident afresh and laughed at ourselves for quite a while before going back to sleep. The next morning, the whole family had a good laugh at us, the girls who had mistaken midnight snacking for Pasikdar's presence. However, since 1990, no midnight noises were worthy of laughter anymore.

THE DOOR ON THE FLOOR

'WHEN JAHAZ USED TO FLY over us during the '65 war, they'd emit a pungent gas that made it difficult for us to breathe. *Yuhoi* tear gas *hyu*. All of us would be lying flat on our stomachs and place large pails of water next to us. In Kashmir, being war-ready is a prudent way of living. It was then that your grandfather and Father decided that we'd keep the ground floor of our home bare. War-ready. You never know. We shifted all the utensils to the first floor. And somehow, living upstairs alleviated my asthma condition too. Then we got used to living there.'

Thus, Bobeh would patiently explain the past to me whenever I expressed curiosity about us not living on the ground floor like the rest of our neighbours. The ground floor fascinated me: to step out of one's house, not into the courtyard, but to be free, to be outside and roam carefree on the streets, uninhibited. But that was not for us.

After the Indo–Pak war of 1965, the ground floor of our house was made unsuitable for everyday living. Part of it had been rented out to a confectioner. The remaining space comprised a kitchen, a large room and a compact *sraan kutth*. The large room was meant for Ramzan Kaak: he kept his belongings there and it was also his bedroom. The ground floor didn't have large or tall windows like in the rest of the house but a few small and ornate roshan daan instead. These windows were meant more for ventilation than anything else. When the warm sunlight peered in during the summer, the shadows of the patterned windows created geometric impressions on the red-oxide floor. It was a struggle for the natural light to enter the ground floor as abundantly as the rest of the house and this made the ground floor appear even more cave-like.

The large, dark room led to a darker corridor which opened on to our pebbled courtyard. Between the corridor and the courtyard stood a colossal storeroom, locally called gaan. The gaan housed sacks full of hundreds of kilos of rice which came from the paddy fields in Parnewa, and large drums filled with copious quantities of coal to be used for kanger in winter. The storeroom also had stacks of tall and trimmed wooden logs which were used to boil water on a mud stove called daan during the winter, especially when the power supply was curtailed, sometimes for weeks at a stretch. The ground floor supplies nourished us during the unpredictable months. From the courtyard outside the storeroom, a large staircase led up to the first floor of our house. That's where the life of the house existed: we cooked, ate, studied, hosted guests, prayed and slept here.

By living on the first floor, in contrast to other houses in the neighbourhood, everything seemed to happen from a distance. I believe that exclusion led me to develop a habit of peering into peoples' homes whose rooms and kitchens opened directly on to the streets or the narrow by-lanes connected to them. The copper and steel utensils in those rooms shone brightly on the green shelves against the walls of their kitchens and living rooms painted in glossy blue paint. The glow of the yellow light that emanated from those rooms suffused me with a feeling of warmth and an inexplicable joy.

To make up for the lost excitement of living like that, we had voggeh. 'At least we have that,' I used to think as a child. Voggeh was a trapdoor. It was a part of our kitchen on the first floor, which opened into a dingy, narrow staircase leading on to the dark room or the bomb-shelter of the 1960s.

To me, it was a mysterious portal and, at times, frightful. Sometimes, an aluminum pail filled with a man's clothes appeared. It felt like a magic trick, as if the mound of clothes had floated upwards on its own. It looked spooky until the enormous figure of Ramzan Kaak emerged from the voggeh as well. When I was much younger and wouldn't listen to Hina, she threatened to push me into the passage from voggeh where I would be trapped forever. The image of being pushed through it would drive me to tears.

It wasn't just me, the voggeh turned out to be equally intriguing to the troops during crackdowns. The first time there was a crackdown in our area, we had to miss both our breakfast and lunch. Aside from the strange memory of hunger and panic, there were three sights that left their mark in our house: The look on the faces of the troops upon discovering the voggeh, the look on the face of Ghaffur, our neighbour, and the look of our house after the troops had left.

It was during one winter morning in 1990. Ramzan Kaak had gone out to buy bread but was sent back in by the troops even before the announcement was made. The announcement, usually made twice, in Urdu and in sometimes Kashmiri, sounded more like a threat: *'Apne gharoon se baahar nikaliyey. Koi aadmi ghar pe na paaya jaaye.'*

Mother, Bobeh and I huddled in our living room, while Ramzan Kaak and Father left the house to be assembled in a large ground of a public school nearby, alongside all the other men from the neighbourhood. The morning passed in a daze, punctuated with the abrupt thuds of doors being slammed and the sound of steel utensils being flung about. Later, of course, these would become the all too familiar 'crackdown noises'.

That morning we felt completely numb, unable to move around; we didn't get any work done, nor speak to each other. The trepidation of our turn being next induced a sickness. I felt constantly nauseous. Towards afternoon, the troops walked into our courtyard. Mother and Bobeh turned paler upon seeing them. I too must have looked like them. I do remember feeling dizzy and light-headed.

Suddenly, the appearance of our frail neighbour, Ghaffur, added some confusion to the already tense situation. Why was he with them? Both Mother and Bobeh wore a quizzical expression upon seeing him. I too was thoroughly puzzled to see Ghaffur with the troops. But I didn't dare to ask anyone anything. The expression on his face was unforgettable. He looked almost dead, like a body that was barely breathing. His face had ashened, and his lips were taut and white.

After the troops walked into our kitchen wearing muddy boots, soiling everything, they flung open the cabinets. Upon discovering the trapdoor on the floor – the voggeh – they went berserk! They ran amok with suspicion, as if they'd unearthed a tunnel to the other side of Kashmir, in Pakistan. Quickly, they broke into two batches: one group cordoned off the house from the outside in the courtyard and the other lot disappeared into the voggeh, into what they seemed to assume to be an imaginary escape tunnel. They did not expect it to be an ordinary floor of an ordinary home with ordinary things. They ventured into the ground floor vehemently, and because they couldn't find anything there, they ransacked the gaan. Suspecting militants to be in hiding behind the gunny sacks, they poked the bayonets of their rifles into them. They slashed open the large rice bags, callously unleashing rivers of grains on to the part-stone, part-mud storeroom floor. They scattered chunks of coal that were hoarded in large tin drums by overturning them. Perhaps it was the adrenaline from discovering the mysterious door that had led them nowhere, or their hurt pride and disappointment for not having recovered any arms, ammunition or even militants from our house. When they left, they left behind nothing but misery that was pasted on to the floors and walls of our house. A misery that couldn't be wiped away.

Since that first time, Mother remained stoic when the troops searched our house. Soon after they'd leave, she'd take stock of the destruction and then, break down. That afternoon, however, seeing our storage room turned upside-down, we succumbed to a deep despair after. To clean up after the crackdown wasn't easy. While the scattered wooden logs could be picked up and stacked back into tall columns, the task of separating bits of coal from rice grains brought me to tears of helplessness and frustration.

Eventually, as the frequency of crackdowns went up over the months and then years, our family broke an age-old tradition and we started storing less grain to avoid the misery of dealing with swathes of strewn paddy. As a thirteen-year-old, I could not fully comprehend what Father and Mother must have gone through. It must have been agonizing to choose between a full storeroom that would sustain the family during long periods of curfew and keeping a less-stocked up room so that we wouldn't end up losing a lot after the troops had unleashed their wrath on our future meals.

That day in 1990, when Father and Ramzan Kaak returned in the evening, we heaved a sigh of relief. Father didn't speak much. Ramzan Kaak told us how the men were paraded in front of a Gypsy that had an informer sitting inside, whose job was to identify militants and militant suspects. The latter could be anybody. All of this would be routine in a few months. That day, as Father locked the house, he remarked on the uselessness of bolts and doors. Even I had understood by then that their safety was by no means guaranteed and that just because the men had been assembled, there was no assurance that they'd return together or return at all.

Each time a house was searched and was found 'clean' – that is, no arms or ammunition was recovered – a date was inscribed on the facade of the house, usually near the main gate. Our house, being in the heart of downtown, had accumulated nine such dates in less than four months.

I MISS WALKING

IT WAS TIME FOR THE dusk-to-dawn curfew to be lifted and for life to resume. Expecting relatives to drop in soon for the funeral, Mother gave three wicker baskets to Ramzan Kaak and asked him to buy bread girde, lawase and baker-khani. She also asked him to drop by at Bibi and Moghel's to request them to come over as soon as they could to help her prepare kahwe with milk and cardamoms for the guests, especially after the burial.

Still numb and in a lifeless state from the thought of parting with Bobeh forever, I was momentarily shaken off from my stupor by the whiff of freshly baked bread from Kandur, the local baker. I followed the aroma and went closer to it into the room where my tutor, Gopi Nath Kaul, used to teach me. The room overlooked the street and a part of the quaint bakery was visible from there.

I sat down, in front of my desk, and looked at the mindless scratches I'd made with a compass, in a state of frustration, a year ago in the autumn of 1993. I'd raise the compass to a height and drop it on the wooden surface of the desk. Sometimes, it'd get stuck on the plank, peel off the off-white paint. Sometimes, it'd skid on the painted surface and create a long scratch. My frustration on that particular morning arose from the fact that I desperately wanted to go for a walk, but could not because the night curfew was yet to be lifted. The aroma of bread being baked was wafting indoors from the baker's and it heightened my urge to go outdoors, walk around, sit beside Tandoor or follow Father to the shrine of Shah Hamdan. Instead, I carved three words with the compass on the surface of the desk and shaded the craters with a pencil. The words I'd written were: 'MORNING WALK, NOW'.

Funnily enough, sitting on my study desk I was reminded of an essay we used to be asked to often write in the school, approximately when we were eight or nine years of age. Our teacher would provide us with essay topics and we would have to write a few paragraphs on it. There was one titled 'A Morning Walk'. Back then, writing that essay bored me. I could not comprehend why we had to write full sentences on the everyday, mundane activity of walking, let alone dense paragraphs. At the age of sixteen, however, unable to go outdoors, I went back to that essay, this time, writing it in quite a different form.

> *Why are people okay with not walking?*
> *Does Father not miss his daily walks to the shrine and his shop?*
> *What about Mother and her long walk to her parents' home?*
> *Does Bobeh not get bored now that she can't kill time watching people walk on the streets?*
> *What happened to my sister who lived her life outside; going to college with her friends, walking long distances to make umpteen visits to her tailor?*
> *I miss playing hopscotch on the streets.*
> *I miss walking in the courtyards and the run to buy kyencza.*
> *Why can't I play hide-and-seek with Mogli's daughter in our courtyard again?*
> *Who walks in the by-lanes, on the bridges, outside the school?*
> *Who can walk to the bakeries?*
> *These are not built for walking.*
> *Left, right, left.*

Then, there was a walk that changed the way I walked forever. At the age of thirteen, my spine curved between my shoulders and my entire upper back often felt tense. A dull ache began then and it persisted.

'Bus No. 1', the school bus that ferried me home, used to be a unique one. Unlike other buses that followed a fixed route to pick and drop students off, our bus alternated between two routes. One route was through the interiors of Shehr-e-Khaas: it started by turning right from the large but dull building of the civil secretariat, passed the bright posters displayed on the façade of Neelam Cinema, snaked into the old quarters of the city, past the shrine of the Sufi saint Syed Mansoor, over the fragile bridge of Nawab Bazar, and then went past the old houses with slim bricks that reeked of the past affluence of their owners. Then, it furthered into the narrow streets outside the historic Pathar Masjid, turned left towards the local police station, finally arriving at Pandit Zind Lal's mammoth spice shop at the mouth of Zaene Kadal.

The second route went straight from the civil secretariat building and made a long-winded drive through the suburbs of the city. It had patches of a good view.

Choosing the route not only depended on the mood of Feroz, the designated bus driver, but also on the students' ability to cheer loudly for their preferred route. Approaching the fork on the road, the driver would deliberately slow the bus down to build anticipation. He would be surrounded by two groups comprising two to three girls each, cheering for either route. Some would climb on to the hot engine to shout right into his ear. While he slowed his pace, at the critical junction, we screamed our lungs out:

'Beminaaaaaaa!'

'Zainaaa Kadaaaal!'

'Beminaaaaaaa!'

'Zainaaa Kadaaaaal!'

Three of us would shout relentlessly: Lubna Samad, Renuka Bazaz and I. Lubna sometimes gave up, but Renuka and I would play the game till its end. In the classroom too, Renuka and I competed over our grades. So it was great fun to clash over the routes on the bus. Depending the direction towards which the wheel steered, one of the two groups would retreat silently, disappointed. They would scamper away towards the seats at the back, expecting the journey to be extended by at least an hour. On the other hand, the ones who'd influenced the driver's decision positively would take the front seats, excited about reaching home earlier, probably getting more time to play, read or just laze about.

All the excitement came to an end in the summer of 1990 when we went back to school briefly after seven months. Renuka was neither in the classroom nor on the bus. I didn't know if she had left in December, like Laxmisree Kaul, or in January, like the rest, but I knew that I would not be seeing her again. Whenever school was open, the driver wouldn't indulge us anymore, but tended to follow a set route like other boring buses. Detours were caused by the news of cross-firing or if an area was under a crackdown.

On one rare day, our school bus reached the Boher Kadal bus stop without many detours. I wanted to visit Father's shop to get my daily pocket money from him, and so I alighted there along with two other girls. It was eerily quiet for an afternoon. Being a part of the bustling business district, Boher Kadal used to be a busy junction, but that day it was dotted with 1-Ton army trucks and other armoured vehicles. The shutters of some shops were rolled down while some had theirs half open. The two other girls, Sabia and Sania, who were sisters and much younger to me, lived nearby. Sabia, the younger one, with a freckled nose and curly, red hair started sobbing. Sania held her hand tightly, looked towards the street, stiffened their gait and walked hurriedly into a narrow alley. They both disappeared from my sight. I was all by myself. The streets I walked every day suddenly seemed threatening.

I had about a kilometre to walk from Father's shop to reach home. On an ordinary day, I'd usually go to Father's shop, barely a minute-long walk from the bus stop, to take some money from him and buy chestnuts or besrakh, that I would eat on my way home. I had to be careful about not eating too much on the way as Bobeh would wait with steaming hot rice and mutton curry for me in a kyenz.

That day, I felt as if I had no legs, as if they had been blown off. Slowly, I walked to the half-shut shop of ours and saw neither Father nor Ramzan Kaak inside. My heart sank. There was no one on the streets whom I could have asked about their whereabouts. All the men had probably been assembled somewhere. There were just the troops around. And what would I ask them? *Have you seen my father?* How does one even talk to the men in uniform?

I could hear my heartbeat outside of my body with warm tears welling up my eyes. My vision blurred. I took my school bag down from my shoulders and hugged it instead. On the deserted streets of my neighbourhood, in the presence of so many military bunkers and the gaze of the unknown men inside them, I suddenly became aware of my body and its contours. My breasts had just assumed their distinct, slightly protruding shape. I felt naked. I tried to fold into the school bag clutched in front of me. That was how I developed a hunch in my upper back.

After I reached home in a rather dazed state, I packed a wide dupatta into my school bag. Since then, I never left home without a chador that could cover my body.

That evening, when Father and Ramzan Kaak returned, I didn't spend time with them. I wrote instead. I traced the spots from Father's shop to our house, the stretch I had somehow managed to walk through physically unharmed that day. But for the future, I created a map with words that I intended to always carry with me even when my mind froze in fear.

Zaene Kadal house = Hear jackboots patrolling at five-thirty.

Boher Kadal shop = Bus stop and the spot where some militants were released in exchange of Rubaiya Sayeed. She hugged her father who protected her because he could.

1/ When I go straight: Navyut = The bus doesn't stop there anymore. There is no one to pick from the big Kawoosa House. Their daughters and I always competed on the number of windows our houses had. I miss showing off to them. They were forced to vacate as the Indian army took over their house. They turned it into a big bunker.

2/ If I turn left: Saraf Kadal = Close to Razey Kadal, an alternate stop for the school bus to pick us up from, if the usual stop is inaccessible due to crackdown.

3/ If I turn right: Navid Kadal = I never keep any memories from that area. They'd parade my father in front of Mukhbirs there.

DAWN

FORBIDDEN COURTYARD

'UNTIL SHE REACHES HER FINAL home, I hope it stays clear like this. It seems like soanth.'

I heard Mother speak next to me as I peeped through the window. It was the kind of dawn that could easily get mistaken for spring. It was neither freezing nor did it wear the bleak shroud of a winter morning. But it couldn't have been spring. More than the palpable turn of air, of the days turning warmer – more pleasant, less chilly – and the less frequent use of kanger during the day, in our home, spring was usually announced with anecdotes by Mother.

Mother would feel nostalgic every time she narrated tales from her childhood, especially of their family picnics to Badam Vaer (the almond cove). I'd always confuse the name with 'Badaem Bagh', but she'd correct me: 'Badam Vaer is not the same as the army cantonment! It's a serene picnic spot with lush almond blossoms.'

'We would take a dyeg full of maccze kebab and a large pot full of rice with us. Toath was fond of condiments, so we would make many kinds – from walnuts, mint, red chillies, to radish and yoghurt. After lunch, while our parents prayed and then rested under the cool shade of the almond blossoms, my sisters and I'd make garlands for them. We kept them aside and played for a bit. Before the evening nun chai, we'd garland Father and make Mother wear our handmade flower bracelets. Father would give us a poand each before we left for home.'

Though it was the same story that Mother told us every year, only with slight variations, I'd feel the soothing breeze of Badam Vaer afresh each spring. I preferred the arrival of spring that way to the other, which also announced spring in our home. That was harsher than Mother's memory. It was through chilli fumes.

Every year in spring, we ground spices at home. A tall, slender wooden log, muhul, was used like a pestle to grind spices in a giant mortar made of stone, called kanz. It sat in a corner of our pebbled courtyard throughout the year, next to the lone Jacaranda tree. Spring was the only season when the kanz was put to its actual use – a receptacle in which to grind spices. At other times, it collected lilac flowers from the tree. Occasionally, it doubled as my safe. Especially when I needed to ask Bobeh for more money to buy candies, I'd hide the coins I had from the previous days in it and place a small stone over them. However, the best use for the kanz had to be during winter, when fresh snow gathered inside it. Since snow remained pristine inside it, I'd scoop out the top layer, add fresh milk and sugar to it, and make scrumptious homemade ice-cream. It felt strangely pleasurable to have chilled things on chilly winter mornings.

Pleasure aside, the kanz made us tearful. Forceful blows on the mounds of dried, crisp chillies in it led to an unending string of sneezes. The task was carried out by two part-time helps: delicate Bibi and enormous Moghel. Both wore long and worn-out pherans, and looked like combatants dressed for a battle. With their faces masked and their hair wrapped under their bandanas, the only facial feature of theirs that was visible was the red rim of their tortured, smarting eyes. They started early and finished late. They lived nearby, behind the cluster of our ancestral houses, in a string of small hutments. The neat rows of their modest housing always smelt of aromatic, fresh chalk paint.

Every spring, during the spice-grinding ritual, other courtyard activities, including me playing House with Bibi and Moghel's daughters, were suspended. The beginning of the ritual mostly caught me unawares. I'd return from school and upon opening the main door, I'd be hit by the unbearable acrid smell of chilli. With my eyes stinging from kreth and a discomfort lodged deep in my throat, I'd drop my satchel downstairs and almost fly to the first floor. On a regular day, that time was the culmination of my walk from the bus stop, the most relaxed part of a school day. I usually dragged my school bag up the staircase listlessly. But on days the chilli-grinding exercise was on, I'd rush upstairs to escape the sudden suffocation from the fumes.

Those days, upstairs turned into a dark chamber. The wooden windows were shut to keep the fumes out. Wanting the arduous affair to end, I'd hold my breath and open a window ever so slightly to peek at the large patterns of chilli spread out on tens of double-spread newspaper sheets. The fumes hung in the air for some time even after the ritual ended. The sting in our eyes and throats stayed even longer.

The last time this ritual was carried out in our courtyard was in the spring of 1989. In fact, any chore that needed to be spread over a few days had to stopped after 1989 simply because it wasn't plausible. Preparing thirty to fifty kilos of chillies, to last an entire year, didn't make sense anymore – an area could be cordoned off by troops for an impromptu crackdown, or be turned into a makeshift thoroughfare by militants. It was more practical to take the spices to a local mill where they'd be ground in machines. Mother preferred to get certain things done in traditional ways, but did she have a choice?

And just like that, our courtyards changed.

They seemed a part of many places that were forbidden to us. The sting was no longer restricted to spring, but from 1990 onwards, it transcended seasons. The sting was of a different kind. When thousands of unarmed dissenters took to the streets to protest the Indian rule, troops fired bullets on these large processions. Sometimes, they fired tear gas. The tear gas entered all homes. Through crevices, gaps, windows ajar, even those that were tightly shut, it entered our rooms and made breathing difficult for the young and laborious for the old. Often, it was worse than the old springtime kreth from chilli fumes.

Next to the houses of Bibi and Moghel, also lived the octogenarian priest, Noori sa'ab. He'd often sit by his window, which opened on to a public courtyard. It was a comforting sight to see him by his window, in a meditative state, with his eyes shut, or sometimes watch him observe the neighbourhood children play after the Asr prayers. After 1990, Noori sa'ab's window hardly ever opened and we learnt that his health had deteriorated rapidly due to the noxious fumes which gathered repeatedly in the public courtyard to which his window opened.

It became a common story. One of my aunts who lived in Khanyar, a restive area in downtown Srinagar, often complained that she felt that her lungs were on fire. '*Zanneh tchum shishnoar dazaan,*' she would say on the phone while breathing heavily, helplessly.

She had developed severe respiratory problems over the years. Somehow, her body could never learn to deal with the sinister blue smoke. The older she turned, the more difficult it became for her to inhale it. When tear gas seeped into our homes, we'd wear a resigned look on our faces and occasionally abuse out loud, '*Trath peynakh!*' But none of us knew how to console my toddler nephew who'd choke on the prickly air as soon as it entered indoors. His cherubic face would turn redder and his eyes would rarely be visible behind a thick film of tears. He'd cry bitterly, unable to articulate how he felt as he gasped for breath.

'This zulm is worse than the war of 1965,' Bobeh whispered to herself each time she saw two-year-old Moosa suffer like that.

SURAH FHEEL: FAITH IN THE FAITH

THE ROOM WAS ABUZZ WITH Quranic verses. I didn't remember many to recite for Bobeh. I hadn't had a tutor to teach me the Quran unlike Hina, who had lessons twice a week before her wedding to prepare her for the customary recital ceremony as a new bride at her husband's house. Surah Al-Fatihah and chaar Qul helped me get by in the month of Ramzan or, when I prayed occasionally on Friday afternoons, upon Mother's insistence.

Surah Al-Fatihah and chaar Qul are a part of every namaaz, but Bobeh would say that, besides namaz-e-janaza (special funeral prayer), Al-Fatihah and Surah Ikhlaas, one of the chaar Qul was also recited at a grave after which a short dua was made for the deceased for their eternal peace.

'*Toath boazi ni amih patih kiheen,*' she would add, telling us that the soul of the departed briefly descend to the earth when we offer a prayer at their graves. She insisted that if we wanted to ask for help from our late grandfather, we should make the plea first, followed by the Surah, as even a soul can recognize that the Surah is the parting prayer.

So, that dawn, I avoided reciting those specific verses while she was still around the house, even if not alive. I didn't want to make it the final goodbye just yet. Instead, I recited Surah Fheel. I recited it over and over again, despite knowing that it was not best suited for the occasion. Surah Fheel was traditionally recited to possess the power of protection from one's enemy, but by 1994, reciting it came to me almost involuntarily. I had learnt it under the circumstances I couldn't shake off: in 1991, when I, along with Ramzan Kaak, was caught in cross-firing, I had recited sections of it. I didn't remember it fully then. I haven't forgotten it since.

'Go to Hina's home. You have hardly been to school this year,' Mother said one day, crinkling her forehead, worried about me skipping school.

It was the summer of 1991, and I had already missed many school days due to the curfew and perpetual unrest in our area.

After her marriage, Hina lived with her in-laws in the Civil Lines, which was uptown and closer to my school.

'At least, the restrictions there are less severe,' Mother went on, packing my haversack. 'Hina says that in case of emergencies, cars do ply there. And curfew passes are not torn by the military as is the case here.' Mother continued mumbling as she kept adding things I needed to carry along with me into the bag. 'Besides, there are fewer soldiers manning the lanes and alleys there. Not like here, where they seal the areas so no one gets in or out. They have to ... All the ministers live there ... They want to tell them that everything is under control.'

I peeped inside the bag and found that besides *Little Women* and *Oliver Twist*, Mother had also packed a large packet of dried apricots. I slipped some notebooks in on which I could sketch faces as I pleased, away from the hawkish surveillance of Bobeh, who was against me drawing faces, as by doing so I was challenging the Creator and therefore committing a grave sin.

Due to Bobeh's prohibition, I had developed a serious handicap in contouring noses. Especially an aquiline Kashmiri nose. I saw an opportunity to practise my skills at Hina's house. With clothes, books and snacks packed for what looked like a week-long stay, I was entrusted in the safe hands of Ramzan Kaak. He was supposed to return on the same day, if circumstances permitted.

I wore my favourite capris, the colour of potassium permanganate, and a long T-shirt. I borrowed one of Mother's chikkankari dupattas and wrapped my head and torso well with it. Usually a thirty-minute ride, we were mentally prepared to spend anything up to three hours in the rickshaw. It would depend on the number of detours we'd have to take, given that some areas would have inevitably been inaccessible because of crackdowns, and some routes dangerous due to a cross-firing battle or a grenade blast – the journey would be constantly lengthening. Despite being aware of such possibilities, Mother took a brave chance to send me off to Hina's.

Barely ten minutes into our rickshaw ride, Ramzan Kaak and I were witnesses to a colossal commotion near the big bunker at Navyut, the area next to Jama Masjid. The tumult also implied that the journey forward wouldn't be possible. Gunshots echoed and a few seconds later, our eyes started smarting from the bluish hue in the air. We saw a few Baktar Band vehicles in the distance and a small crowd running in our direction. It seemed as if they would collide into our vehicle, crushing us under their collective weight.

'*Wapas pheyr sa hye, ati tchuui jang chalaan!*'

At least four people screamed those words, urging everyone to turn around and escape the war zone, while running in different directions for their lives. I thought I saw a couple of young men with guns slung across their bodies. Had I seen militants for the first time? Or were they the aides? But they had guns! We were caught between the tear gas being fired from one side, and the cross-firing between militants and troops on the other. I turned numb, besides finding it impossible to breathe. I expected to be a hit by a shell or a bullet. Why wasn't it hitting us already? When would that moment be? I could only think of bullets. I could almost see them.

The rickshaw driver and Ramzan Kaak were discussing about which route to take back, but I could not follow anything.

Then, somehow, I managed to mumble verses from Surah Fheel, incoherently, mixing the lines up. By reciting them in a different order, I was perhaps asking for the opposite. I don't know. Bobeh often said it has the power to protect one against the enemy. Was I even asking for that?

O Beloved! Have you not seen how your Lord
Dealt with the companions of the Elephant?
Did He not make their plan into misguidance?
And He sent against them birds in flocks,
Striking them with stones of hard clay,
And He made them like eaten straw.

The verses told the story of a brave flock of swallows, who carried little balls of baked clay in their beaks to attack the enemy and protect Ka'aba during one of the battles mentioned in the Quran. I was struggling to remember the lines. As the rickshaw negotiated its way through multiple by-lanes, I made a promise to myself: 'If I survive today, Surah Fheel would be the first thing I'd recite each time upon leaving home.'

Sitting near Bobeh's motionless body and reciting the verses, I wondered why on that fateful day three summers ago, it was the Surah Fheel that had come to my mind. Maybe I had thought that the power of verses might prompt the birds flying over Navyut to protect us.

I WOULD GROW UP TO BE COLLATERAL DAMAGE

THE LIGHT OF THE MORNING was expanding. It was getting brighter. The softest, most measured footsteps could be heard coming from the direction of the main door, and I knew who it was: Aunt Nelofar. Considerate as always, Father's youngest sister, my aunt Nelofar walked in quietly and hugged Father. They both sobbed quietly. Aunt Nelofar's presence made me aware of the sombreness of the funeral that would begin in a few hours. I recalled the funeral Aunt Nelofar had been to a few months ago, the one that she kept referring to as Karbala.

It was raining hard that day. I was covering my new textbooks with brown paper. It had been four months since our exams had been over, but the results were not out yet as the year had been especially restive. Teachers couldn't work. As this was considered one of the most crucial years of high school, Father thought I should not waste time and get started with the syllabus on my own. Assuming I would pass, he bought me a new set of books for the next grade. Then, as usual, our annual squabble began: he wanted to give the books to the binder to get them hardbound and I didn't want to part with my books.

'What if the shop is gutted in a gunfight? What if the owner is killed and they never open the shop again? What if the binder goes missing and never returns?' I worried, selfishly.

'I will cover them with brown paper and then wrap cellophane on top,' I convinced Father.

He didn't try to reason too much. He wasn't aware of what I was thinking. He bought me some sheets of brown paper, cellophane and a large bottle of glue. I was short of one roll of brown paper to cover some of my notebooks. I decided to cover the remaining ones with newspapers until schools opened regularly that year, which was a matter of chance than anything else. I looked through piles of broadsheets in the storage under the staircase. Though the writing in Urdu looked appealing and calligraphic, it also meant wrapping notebooks with unending deaths, killings, arrests and protests printed on those broadsheets. The morbid print was likely to discourage me from opening them.

I opted for the pile of Indian English dailies, which, other than the local news, also carried large sections of full-colour advertisements. These print ads had men posing with colognes, couples grinning wide to show their perfect dentition, young women posing even as they'd wake up in their fluffy beds to morning rays of the sun or slightly older women beaming at their children and their laundry, celebrating their motherhoods and everyday chores alike. I had developed a habit of scrutinizing the ads, wondering about the lives of the people who made them, the ones who featured in them and the people these ads were intended for. It was a world that was far from the long-standing strife and bereft of any unresolved political conflict. I wondered if it knew how, not more than 1,000 kilometres away, it had become commonplace for ordinary people to survive the fallouts of war: losing limbs in grenade blasts and kin to arrests and bullets, contracting splinters, being caught in cross-firings, and seeing their homes turn into battlefields. What kind of advertisements could such everyday routines inspire? Not ones pretty enough to be printed in full-colour, I thought.

The newsprint smiles on the faces of the models in the advertisements made me wonder if I would be a different person altogether had I grown up away from a conflict zone, outside of a disputed territory. To wake up to the rays of the sun without having the previous night's sleep interrupted by screams of the neighbourhood women who'd run after the armed personnel in convoys that took away their husbands and teenage sons in nocturnal raids. To only care about using the right colognes and worry about the right detergent, to not to have to constantly think about the availability of vegetables, milk and medicine during erratic but long periods of curfew ... I wondered what life would be like if there was some certainty in our day-to-day affairs. Wouldn't that be wonderful? Felt more like a dream...

Meanwhile, outside, it continued to pour. I was adrift as I was slowly wrapping my books with the newspapers. That is when Aunt Nelofar paid us a visit all of a sudden. She was drenched. As she had come straight from a funeral, she looked even more dishevelled.

She took her soaked dupatta off and asked me to iron it dry. While I plugged the iron in, Mother got her a cup of dalcheen kahwe. She began telling us what was weighing on her mind.

'Three days ago, the younger sister of Tanveer, the one who teaches economics in my new college, came to visit her in the college during lunch break. I was walking past them, when Tanveer introduced me to her and told me she was the one who had recently been engaged. I congratulated her and kissed her forehead. The lunch break was about to end, so I rushed back to the staff room leaving the sisters to themselves. The rest of the staff members were already getting ready to resume their afternoon classes...

'As we dispersed, suddenly, there was a loud bang. The glass panes of our staff room rattled. It felt like the room was going to cave in with that immense shock. We could hear students shriek. A bomb had gone off in Regal Chowk, just outside the college. Tanveer's sister had stepped out after their meeting. Just when the blast had occurred. She was killed in the blast. But that's not it...

'They struggled to look for her remains ... she had been blown into smithereens and had to be identified by the tatters of her clothing that hung from the electrical wires just outside the college.'

I finished ironing Aunt Nelofar's dupatta dry. The newspapers lay scattered on the living room floor.

SHADOW OF A SIEGE

AUNT NELOFAR STARTED REMOVING THE accessories off Bobeh to ready her for the final bath. She carefully loosened her mother's tokke kor from her wrist, removed the coral ring from the ring finger of her right hand, as if not to hurt her, as if Bobeh were still alive. It was the ring that Bobeh had promised to give me as a present if I scored a distinction in my school leaving exams, the previous year, in 1993.

'If you graduate with a distinction, I'll get you gold earrings that are bigger than I gave your sister,' Mother had promised me. Father had promised to buy me a camera. Other relatives were expected to give token money as and when they would visit our home to congratulate me after the exam results were declared. There would perhaps be a small party. To celebrate her grades, a distant cousin had her ears pierced in the presence of guests. Another one got engaged during her celebratory party as her would-be mother-in-law was smitten by her beauty on the day of the function. Graduating with a distinction was life-changing in many ways. While I was not inclined to get engaged or to have my ears pierced (I had mine done many years ago), I was looking forward to taking the big decisions of life. I was getting impatient to plan my life beyond high school. I was excited to finally give up studying subjects that I lacked interest in. I wanted to read Urdu for pleasure and not necessarily to pass exams or secure good grades.

'Matric pass' connoted a new life, a passage to freedom. Thereafter, one could choose to be anything: doctor, engineer, lawyer, lecturer! The azadi to choose one's destiny! It was also for the first time that we could compete with the students across the valley and Ladakh, though not the entire state. The school term in Jammu had a different academic calendar from ours. Even though the board or the state exams were not supposed to be as tough compared to the ones held at school, it was the sheer number of pupils appearing for them that made them more exciting and challenging.

Owing to it being another unquiet year, just like the previous two, in 1992, schools across Kashmir had been opened sporadically and all of us struggled to finish our syllabus by ourselves at home. I was not particularly good at physics and had to seek help from my cousin who lived nearby. He would come over to our place to help me out whenever he could, but even that wasn't enough. Indefinite curfew interspersed with civil curfew lasted for days on end. But private tuition or not, I was determined to secure a good percentage. I studied relentlessly.

'Your future depends on these results,' Mother would often say throughout the year. She said it more emphatically on the morning when Ramzan Kaak excitedly announced, as he walked into the living room with a phoat full of bread, *'Date sheet tchu draamut.'*

Looking at my exam date sheet printed in a newspaper, made it a big deal. In fact, I was so excited that I ran a mild fever for a couple of days. But there was worse to come.

It was the first week of December and our exams were to begin soon. Babri Masjid in Ayodhya was demolished. We, in Kashmir, were put under preventive curfew. As if we didn't get enough curfews of our own. It impacted our exams. Postponements and rescheduling! The exams that were supposed to end in ten days took a month and a half to finish. I lost interest in getting a good score. It was difficult to maintain enthusiasm, and the curfews put our willpower to test. I didn't care how well I did. I didn't secure a distinction.

By the time the results came out – five months after they were supposed to – my excitement had dried up completely. The gifts promised to me by my family members were forgotten. There was no celebratory lunch at our house, not because of my grades (they were not shameful!) but the fact that between December 1992 and April 1993, another tragedy befell us.

After a gun-battle in Lal Chowk, near Palladium cinema, troops had set ablaze an entire patch of shops. My maternal aunt's husband and some more relatives owned a few of them.

It was in the wake of that misfortune that Bobeh encouraged me to do better the next year. '*Ye vaejj dime tczey,*' she promised to give me the heirloom ring again. The promise didn't stir anything in me.

It seemed like the time of the exams had become jinxed. In October 1993, a month before the dates were announced for the final exams, militants had taken refuge in the Hazratbal shrine.

'It is going to be Karbala this time. May Parvardigaar keep all of us in His safe custody,' Mother sighed. 'When Moi-e-Muqadas was stolen in the 1960s, thousands of people took to the streets. People would gladly lay their lives to protect the relic of their beloved Prophet (peace be upon him). Thankfully, it had miraculously reappeared after two weeks on its own.'

With the siege and subsequent desecration of the mosque, despair and panic found their way into every house in our neighbourhood. Bobeh sobbed ceaselessly on her prayer rug. Father and Ramzan Kaak remained glued to the transistor radio for news updates.

The siege lasted for around forty days.

It involved prolonged negotiations between the militants and the government. Every other day, there were new demands from the militants and the state laid out new conditions. People, as expected, took to the streets, but the dense militarization ensured they did not reach Dargah. Scores of unarmed protestors were killed and injured that October near Vejbyoar.

Unsure of the outcome and the uncertainty that prevailed around the siege, I had lost the resolve to do well in my exams. What was the point? People were struggling to stay alive. How did my distinction matter? The round-the-clock curfew, the killings, the protests, the futile dialogues, the labelling of men sometimes as militants, sometimes as mercenaries ... the constant shifting of power had done its damage. I didn't know then, but it was the beginning of an apathy for my own self that would last for a long time. Our lives were controlled from elsewhere and the dreams that we dreamt were always at the mercy of someone else, someone occupying us, ruling us. The red of the coral of Bobeh's ring just did not appeal to me anymore.

CINEMAS? NO SCOPE!

AT AROUND EIGHT O'CLOCK, HINA'S friend and our distant relative, Neelam and her mother brought a large samovar of dodh kahwe and a few wicker baskets full of bread for us, the bereaved.

Neelam and my sister Hina were friends since childhood. She lived nearby. I was fascinated with her name since Neelam also happened to be the name of a popular cinema in Srinagar.

I chuckled whenever she visited Hina. Then the funnier thing happened. When Neelam was getting married, Hina's vocabulary was suddenly reduced to two words: Neelam and Nikah. A trip to the tailor for an outfit for Neelam's Nikah. An appointment with the beautician for Neelam's Nikah. It was hilarious that Hina seemed busier than the bride, perhaps obsessing over her outfits and accessories for the wedding.

Those two words were of great importance to me because of other reasons. *Nikaah* was the first Indian film I had watched in Neelam Cinema. I was around six then.

The cinema belonged to a distant relative of ours, someone from the maternal side of my family. They had arranged a special screening of *Nikaah* for the immediate and extended family. I remember being dressed in one of the best frocks that I had at that time. It was a sea-green organza dress with tiny paisley motifs at the white hem. The green of my outfit resembled the colour on the facade of the cinema.

Though I barely remembered the film from the screening, I could never forget the curious nature of the evening which was both formal and fun. We were seated in a box, a mini gallery that separated a 'special audience' from the regular cinema goers. We were served tea and snacks during the interval. Most of the relatives who had come for the matinee show were women. All of us watched the entire film without a murmur, unlike the audience who had paid for the tickets. They were whistling and humming along to a ghazal sung by a Pakistani singer, Ghulam Ali.

Chupke chupke raat din aansu bahana yaad hai
Hamko ab tak aashiqui ka woh zamana yaad hai.

When I was around eight or nine years old, Father took me to another cinema, Palladium, to watch an English film. I don't recall the name of the film, but I do remember my reaction when we got back home. Astonished, I told my sister Hina, who was helping me change, 'It didn't have songs!'

'Oh really?' she asked, pretending to sound surprised.

Of course, she was aware of that difference between Indian and foreign films. She revealed that to me much later when I was old enough to be trusted with some of her secrets. She confessed to having bunked many classes during her college days to catch matinee shows, clandestinely.

'I avoided going to Neelam. Chances of being spotted there were higher. Anyone could rat on me and the news would reach home before I did,' she said, raising her eyebrows. 'Palladium was too exposed. College goers hardly went there. So were Broadway and Regal. Especially after Regal played *Lion of the Desert* that had instigated anti-Sheikh Abdullah sloganeering and protests in the '80s. Firdaus cinema was far from home. That left us with four options to choose from: Shah, Naz, Sheraz and Khayyam…' She counted the names off on her fingertips.

In 1990, all the fifteen cinema theatres of the valley shut down. Allah Tigers, one of the many militant outfits, had declared watching films as un-Islamic. They had repeatedly threatened the owners of cinemas until they were compelled to shut shop. After cinemas, video rental libraries were banned too.

Father hid our VCR under Mother's old clothes in a trunk. The trunk was carried to the attic by Ramzan Kaak. It remained there, shut for a few years. With cinemas gone and TV nearly non-existent, transistor radios became essential to stay up to date. It made up for our entertainment needs too. I got hold of an old, orange pocket transistor radio that Father had bought from Hajj. I kept it for myself. By the time I was sixteen, I knew all the old Hindi film songs by heart. I'd tune into a Nepali radio station at one-thirty at night to listen to Hindi songs on a low volume, so as not to disturb Bobeh.

When it came to listening to authentic news bulletins, transistor radios became important as we'd tune into BBC Sairbeen and Voice of America for unbiased coverage from the ground. At night, Father placed a large transistor radio in front of him. The frequency kept drifting into static. Ramzan Kaak would sit in front of him at that hour, his chunky fingers tracing the patterns on the carpet. It was a hassle to tune in to the clearer frequency. Sometimes, in the middle of grim news, it'd catch some Hindi film song and we wouldn't know what to make of that irony. Father kept on dialling into the right frequency.

Once, the newsreader had just uttered the word 'vaardaat', meaning mishap, when the needle jumped to a music station playing a popular Hindi song: '*Shayad phir iss janam mein…*' (in a shrill female singer's voice)

'… vaardaat…' (in a male presenter's baritone)

'… *ho na ho…*' (back to the song).

It was a strange but comical mash-up: A mishap may or may not happen in this lifetime.

As much as transistor radios filled the entertainment gap in our lives, as a teenager I yearned to go to the cinema. Every time our school bus drove past Neelam cinema, I'd see that the troops had taken it over – hundreds of stacked-up sacks, spools of concertina wires, empty liquor bottles were splattered all around it. The fading green on the building's facade would always remind me of a happier time and of the green dress I wore the only time I went through its doors.

A WEDDING, A FUNERAL

Why didn't I arrange for a gun, Baayo?
Why didn't I listen to you, Baayo?
I thought we'd get you out of there soon, Baayo!
What harm had you done to the Mukhbir, Baayo?
I should have arranged for a gun for you, Baayo!
I am responsible for your death, Baayo!
I should have arranged for a gun for you, Baayo!
I should have arranged for a gun for you, Baayo!
Shall I put henna on you, Potro?
Are you thirsty, Potro?
Myani potro, myani potro (my son, my son)

My mother's sister had arrived. She was singing a dirge. It took me back to her son's funeral in 1991. I had seen him a week before he was killed. We were at a wedding.

It was one of the first daytime weddings I had attended. Before 1989, nights were for celebrations and days for funerals. Then curfew took over all our nights, and both mourning and celebrations moved to the days.

In the autumn of 1991, Suraiya, a distant cousin, was getting married. Our fathers had been friends since school, so, all of us were invited. Father, Mother and I went. Bobeh stayed at home as usual. She didn't like crowds much. It worsened her asthma. Her share, a large traem, with about two kilos of meat dishes and rice on it, big enough to feed an entire family, would arrive separately.

As soon as we got there, Mother took charge of the room that had the bride's jewellery and gifts for her in-laws. Father was one of the witnesses at the nikah. He got busy with the technicalities of the marriage contract. From finalizing alimony and deciding thaan (gifts) to the specific timing for the ceremony – he had to help out with delicate matters. I spent time with the bride in her room. Her friends were readying her for the muss miczraven ceremony by braiding her hair with ribbons and colourful thread with ornate tassels to decorate her multiple plaits. They made her look funny, I thought. After the ritual, colourful ribbons would be distributed among girls of marriageable age before the henna ceremony began. I didn't like the gifts that were being arranged for the guests either. The gift tray had cheap combs, ribbons, hair clips, brooches. I pushed it towards the window. The light outside was dimming as the day outside was coming to an end. Suddenly, I felt restless. A strange fear would grip me at the fall of dusk for some indescribable reason. All I wanted to do was to be at home with my family around me. Even though there were all known faces at the wedding, and I wasn't alone, a strange anxiety took hold of me. My throat tightened. My breathing became laboured, as if someone was strangling me. It took effort to breathe normally. All that usually occurred at the onset of twilight during dusk and the symptoms worsened if I wasn't home.

Mother had decided to stay the night, but I wanted to go home.

'Can I please go back?' I pestered her.

'There is hartal. Who is going to drop you? You know your Father is busy. Can you wait for him?' she sounded worked up.

'I can also carry traem for Bobeh with me, you won't have to worry about arranging for it,' I tried to reason.

'But I'll still need to arrange for someone to go with you,' said Mother, visibly irritated.

'What if Father also decides to stay back?' I asked her.

'*Vatti peth tchakheh?* Are you stranded on a road?'

She knew that Father staying back was a possibility. I knew she wouldn't risk letting him leave after the night curfew was imposed.

I sulked. I just couldn't help the restlessness. The tremors in my heart were as real as the tears welling up in my eyes. I was not throwing a tantrum.

Sensing my desperation, Mother started looked around, enquiring if anyone was on their way out. She caught a glimpse of her sister Amina's son.

'Affi jaan! Are you staying here tonight or going back?'

'Why? Do you need something?' he asked.

'This one is missing Bobeh and wants to go home. If you are leaving, can you please drop her on your way?' she requested him, while touching her own chin. It was a gesture of plea.

'Please don't embarrass me like that, Khaali. Of course, I will drop her.'

'Now, you will carry traem for Bobeh or else Father will be upset with you,' Mother said sternly to me.

Hearing this, my cousin Affi interjected, 'No, no, please, no traem! We will have to answer the military at every bunker! At least seven of them by the time we reach Zaene Kadal. With that kind of meat and rice, they'll start a crackdown on the plate and even arrest us until they finish eating all the food. Pack some food in a small tiffin case. How much will Bobeh eat, anyway?'

We set out on his two-wheeler. On our way, he advised me, 'Don't pester your mother again. Parents should be looked after, not troubled. I wasn't going home tonight, but I could sense your mother needed help.'

It didn't take us long from Khanyar. We reached home after being stopped only twice to check his ID at two bunkers near Razze Kadal and Saraf Kadal.

'Come in for a bit?' I asked him, sheepishly. I felt guilty about having troubled him.

'I will visit again soon, I promise. *Boabas venzi salaam.* I must go back and help Suraiya's father. I'm not going home tonight,' he smiled his usual effusive smile. His green eyes shone with kindness. I looked back and remember him riding away in his denim jacket. That was the last time I saw him alive. He was killed a week later.

A week later, his bullet-riddled body, with his bandaged throat, was laid in the middle of their small lawn, outside their home. That was his funeral.

I learnt that his sister Zahida had seen him after he was arrested at a crackdown. The troops had brought him back home.

'*Bondook antai yeman kuni jaai, naatteh hai maarnai mye yem.* Arrange a gun from somewhere, they'll kill me otherwise.'

He had begged her to 'procure a gun' for him as that is what the troops had demanded. That was the last time he had spoken to her. Helpless, she had run after the jeep, begging them to spare her brother's life. His family was just gearing up for a long process to look for him in different jails and apply for his release. The next morning, they awoke to a commotion outside their home. Bullet-pierced bodies of three boys who had been picked up by the troops the previous day, including Affi's, were found outside on the street.

Zahida looked paler than Affi Bhaiya's corpse. She was carrying a tray with almonds and candies on it, as if he were a groom and not a martyr. She had tied her scarf around her waist and was wailing loudly.

Why didn't I arrange for a gun, Baayo?
Why didn't I listen to you, Baayo?
I thought we'd get you out of there soon, Baayo!

What harm had you done to the Mukhbir, Baayo?
I should have arranged for a gun for you, Baayo!
I am responsible for your death, Baayo!
I should have arranged for a gun for you, Baayo!
I should have arranged for a gun for you, Baayo!

For a long time after his killing, my aunt, his mother, would often go missing from her room in the early hours of the day. Her husband and daughter would go out looking for her in the houses of their neighbours or at the local shrine. One such morning, they passed Affi Bhaiya's grave and found her there. She had been frantically trying to dig him out. They took her home. Her husband decided to stay awake at night to guard her. Three weeks later, sometime early in the morning, while keeping an eye on his inconsolable wife, he had gone to help himself to some water either in the kitchen, or had needed to go the washroom. He mistook a window in the corridor for a door and fell to his death.

MORNING

SPEECH IMPEDIMENTS

EVEN AMIDST THE MURMURS OF prayers and conversations which had suffused the entire house, I recognized the source of the heavy grunts coming in from the courtyard. It had to be Koal. He loved Bobeh deeply. He felt the care in her gestures and kindness in her eyes without her expressing any of that in words.

Koal was the deaf-mute part-time help who had been with us for as long as I can remember. Whenever Mother had to ask him to buy milk, she'd put her fists up until her chin, and move them up and down repeatedly, in a parallel motion; it looked like Mother was milking an invisible cow. To buy tczochvoar, Bobeh would put her fists together, fingers facing each other, and then pull them back on either side. It indicated breaking bread. Each task had one or many codes by which we used to communicate with him. He knew many signs, but just one sound that was intelligible: 'Maaley'.

On Sundays, when Father napped in the afternoon, Koal announced his arrival in the courtyard with that sound, 'Maaley'. Irked, Mother would come out and look at him sternly. She pressed her index finger to her lips asking him to hush and followed that up by another gesture of tilting her head towards her right shoulder with her eyes closed, to inform him of Father's siesta. Everyone had their own simple ways to communicate with him, but he and I shared a close and special bond. In my head, at least. I had observed him closely after an incident that almost left me with a speech impairment.

After returning from school, during my playtime, I'd pretend to be a teacher and turn our drawing room into a classroom. I'd rearrange the bolsters and line up the cushions neatly in a row, like desks. The upright bolsters were my students. I too had to look the part. So I raided Mother's cupboard and stole two dupattas. I was often spoilt for choice, as she had dupattas of many colours and fabrics, some embroidered and some beaded, or with tassels, laces, and so on… Mother's fashionable headgears were my favourite props, as they served me well no matter which role I enacted on a particular day. A dupatta could turn into a young girl's long, flowing mane on some days. On others, I'd wrap around the specially embroidered mukaish dupatta around my body to resemble Mrs Iqbal or Mrs Mendoza's sarees. I would also fashion muslin ones into a turban when pretending to be a sage collecting alms, just like I'd seen in one of Mother's photographs from her college annual function.

One afternoon, when I was eight years old, after school and before tuitions, I was standing on the ledge of the window, which was my pretend dais, from where I, the head teacher, was supposed to conduct morning prayers and sing hymns. After that, I would climb down to the floor and walk across to the corner, to an imaginary staff room. Engrossed in my make-believe world, and unmindful of the pencil clenched in my teeth, when I raised my hands up in the air and jumped, I lost balance and fell. The pencil in my mouth hit the floor first and then, the roof of my mouth. It cut the soft membrane of my palate and got stuck there. Panicking, and in pain, I went to the kitchen to look for Mother or Bobeh. At the sight of my mouth full of blood, Mother screamed in horror, *'Taavan ha pyoam!'*

She didn't dare pull the pencil out. 'Take her to Hedwun. I will phone the shop and send someone there,' Bobeh told Mother.

I was lucky since Koal was around on that day. Even though he was of a petite build, he had immense strength. He carried me in his outstretched arms all the way from home, on to a tonga, and let go of me only at in the Emergency ward of the hospital, where I was put on a stretcher and taken inside.

'Either she will resume talking within forty-eight hours, or she'll never be able to talk again,' in a semi-conscious state,

I overheard a doctor telling Father and Mother. Koal was standing nearby, looking equally distressed. The bloodstains on his grey shirt had dried. I also heard the doctor instruct my parents to feed me as much ice-cream as I'd be able to have. At least, there was some good news!

At home, the next two days were spent in apprehension. I was in a strange place. Eating spoonfuls out of the tubs of strawberry, vanilla and pistachio ice-cream, I kept looking at Koal who had stayed around, helping with chores. I was already conjuring images of him and I using the same sign language to communicate with each other and with the rest of the world. I would be able to hear though, I thought. He didn't have that advantage. Like Koal's 'Maaley', with which he addressed every woman, I wondered about the only sound-word I would be able to utter.

However, I was lucky to be able to recover fast and not lose my ability to speak. After the wound in my mouth had healed, I got away with a mild stutter. But that incident made me communicate with Koal more. Sometimes, if I asked him to fetch me something that I wanted urgently, and if he didn't listen to me, I pretended to hold an imaginary rifle at him and to pull its trigger. He would groan like a wounded animal.

What I also realized in those days was that since he couldn't hear, Koal didn't have a name. At least, not one anyone knew of. Koal means someone who cannot speak. Most people would not call him; instead, they signalled at him, gestured with their hands or just tapped on his shoulder. His sole identity was that he was deaf-mute.

After identity cards were made mandatory in 1990, no one paid enough attention to have one made for him. The absence of an ID card meant walking on a minefield. There was a higher possibility of an arrest, an enforced disappearance by the troops. Anyone without an ID on them could easily be detained on the pretext of being a militant suspect.

Koal paid the price for not owning one. One day, as he was sauntering on the street past the evening curfew time, he was stopped by the troops to become their punching bag for that evening. He had incessantly screamed the only word he could, 'Maaley, maaley'. That was when his sister had heard him, his sound-word puncturing the silence of the neighbourhood. She'd rushed outside and pleaded with them to leave her brother alone. She had placed her dupatta at the feet of troops who were hitting him with their rifle butts.

Koal's bruises and broken leg took several weeks to heal, but when they did, he hesitated to step out of his sister's house after dark, even though his sister had an ID card made for him. After that evening, he was unable to make his only sound-word, 'Maaley'.

Even when he mourned for Bobeh, he did so wordlessly.

CURFEW AS POISON

THE FUNERAL RITES GATHERED MOMENTUM – in one corner of the courtyard, water was being heated in a large copper dyeg placed on unevenly cut logs of wood; in another corner, Moghel was adding rose water to another pail of water. Apprentices of professional waza took over a part of the kitchen on the ground floor to prepare food and salty tea for mourners. Neighbours cleaned up the pebbled courtyard to create space for pallbearers who would gather alongside the coffin.

Mother asked me to go upstairs to gather my books, which were lying scattered here and there, and make room for more guests who'd drop by to offer their condolences. Some close ones were expected to stay over because the dusk-to-dawn curfew would be imposed again. I went upstairs to the large room, which was separated by the ornate wooden wurusi that turned it into four big chambers. I entered the one where Bobeh used to sleep. I rolled up her quilt and mattress together, and proceeded to roll mine in the adjacent chamber. I picked up my books which lay by the windowsill and carried them to a free-standing cupboard. Earlier that summer in 1994, I had written a few lines on the inside of its door with a teal chalk that I had stolen from school.

> How I celebrated August 15
> Laid up
> With poison in my belly
> Holed up
> Holding up
> Desperate
> I went out to buy medicines
> Through the narrow lanes
> Roads cut into wedges
> By barbed wires
> Curfew is a poison
> That everyone was fed
> With swollen eyes and my blistered lips
> I saw and read
> Graffiti on the shutters
> Azadi

Curfew and poisoning had things in common is what I realized on 14 August 1994. That summer, they had taken over my life, and held me captive. That day started with a craving. I opened the door of our fridge to the sight of a frozen goshtaab that immediately made me salivate. After letting it thaw, I cut the meatball into two neat halves, like two half-moons, which I further sliced into quarters until I had eight meat wedges in front of me. I fried them crisp and polished them off within minutes. Bobeh always served goshtaab with hung yoghurt. I had skipped that part, and perhaps that was my mistake.

The goshtaab that I had consumed had come from a wedding in the neighbourhood. It was precious in a way. By 1994, wazwaan, the traditional multi-course meal that we all looked forward to, had become scarce because wedding functions were truncated, and the guest lists had become more intimate. There were fewer celebrations and no post-sunset ceremonies. More common in the Pandit culture, the only day-wedding I had been to, was of the granddaughter of my tutor Gopi Nath Kaul, or Mashterji as we'd call him. That was in 1988. Muslim weddings usually took place in the evenings and went on until the early hours of the morning. After 1990, the dusk-to-dawn curfew and nocturnal raids made it impossible to host any celebratory functions after dusk. For the daytime functions, people attended them only if they had to, something they couldn't skip: a wedding or a function which was within the immediate family or at a next-door neighbour's.

Mother had gone to attend one such function somewhere in the extended neighbourhood and had returned within two hours. Under ordinary circumstances, within that duration, guests were only served kahwe, sheermaal, khatai and dry fruits. That was followed by the elaborate feast which went on for at least three to four hours. All that was over.

It was mid-August, and unusually hot. As it happens, one loses their appetite in summer, and Mother hadn't eaten much at the wedding. Besides, it's a tradition to pack some extra food in a plastic bag for the guest to take home. So, she had carried back goshtaab and a couple of kebabs with her. We had kebabs that very day for dinner with a walnut-and-yoghurt condiment that Ramzan Kaak made. Mother kept the meatball for later. She had probably forgotten about it. Until I devoured it, of course!

After my secret, scrumptious meal, a strange lethargy crept into my bones and I fell into a deep sleep. When I woke up, I couldn't get out of bed. Later, I think Bobeh tried to feed me rice porridge as I was drifting in and out of sleep, but I barely had the energy to sit up to swallow it.

I was in pain the whole night. Mother gave me a couple of cups of dalcheen kahwe but didn't feed me anything solid. I could neither vomit nor flush the poison out.

On 15 August, I awoke with a swollen face. Bobeh prepared gulkand. I had it despite the lingering nausea, but the stomach infection had set in too deep by then to be cured by home remedies. Lack of medical attention was making it worse by the hour. By evening, the pressure of the swelling on my eyelids was such that I could barely open my eyes. I occasionally looked around with my half-hooded eyes. Despite my puffed-up face and eyes, expecting worse, I dragged myself out to go with Mother to the house of a nearby chemist and get some medicines for temporary relief until the curfew was lifted and I could see a doctor.

All the shops were shut. The roads were deserted. Every little nook and alleyway had a trooper or two since it was 15 August and we were under strict 'restrictions'. There was no point going ahead and putting ourselves through the unnecessary hassle of walking through the barbed wire only to be turned back. I was in no mood to present my inflamed face to the troops and be at their mercy to decide whether we should be allowed to pass through or not. We turned back. I had no option but to wait out another long day of confinement followed by a dark evening of a power blackout symbolizing the rejection of celebrating India's independence. Through all that, I clutched my stomach and tried to sleep off my pain. A few days later, I recovered, but that date always reminded me of poisoning.

MEMORY OF THE LAKE

'POUR SOME WATER ON HER. You owe it to her. She will feel peaceful,' Mother told me while preparing Bobeh for her final bath.

They moved Bobeh to the kitchen on the first floor. Bibi, my aunts and Mother were there, and a few other close relatives went in and out. So far, I hadn't said a single prayer. I hadn't cried either. Bobeh lay still on a plank of wood. Her fine and surprisingly black hair spread on it like spilt ink. Her mouth was parted as though she was in deep sleep after offering her early morning namaaz. Mother was cleaning Bobeh's nails with a thin twig. I poured water on her hair and her firm shoulders from an aluminium vessel that Bibi handed over to me. Then I walked out rather quickly. My eight-year-old cousin Nida, aunt Nelofar's youngest daughter, was standing alone outside the kitchen. Nida's soft hazel pupils were dilated. She was old enough to understand about the passing of Bobeh but too young to not be overwhelmed by the ambience of mourning. She was fiddling with the black amulet, the taeveez that she wore around her neck. I held her by the hand and took her aside. I tied her soft, golden curls into a bun. Her right hand was around her neck, as if glued to the taeveez. I remembered the first time I saw her fiddle with it in the autumn of 1992 at their home in Nigeen.

Aunt Nelofar, my Father's youngest sister, was a professor by profession. She taught at Nawa Kadal Women's College. With three degrees in Persian literature, she had a knack of weaving in couplets by Saidi and Jami, or Firdausi's *Shahnama*, into mundane conversations, elevating them into something of spiritual significance. She'd also recite from memory the lesser known couplets by Ghalib. With her ability to find fine links between literature and the everyday incidents, she could transform situations like magic. Once, frantically looking for Ramzan Kaak to send him to buy milk from Sobur goor, the local milkman, she broke into a couplet by Ghalib:

> *Sanam sunte hain teri bhi kamar hai*
> *Kahaan hai, kis taraf hai, kidhar hai?*

In 1992, she was transferred to another college, which was farther from our house. Thereafter, she visited us less regularly. Her old college was between our house and the bus depot. The new one was away in the suburbs. When she visited us more often, she'd bring me books and candies. I began missing being spoiled by her, but most of all, I missed listening to her humorous anecdotes and the staff-room gaffes.

She would often recite a couplet for Kashmir.

Har sookhtah-e-jaaniee ki ba' Kashmir dar aayad
Gar murg kebab ast baa baal va par aayad.

'I like Urfi's couplet over the famous one associated with Kashmir,' she would say.

When I asked her why, she said, '*Hameen asto, Hameen asto, Hameen asto* is too popular. No wonder it is mostly used by politicians and tourism advertisements. The one by Urfi speaks more of Kashmir's aab-o-hawa, better captures the seasons and their charms...'

No wonder Aunt Nelofar lived by the banks of the picturesque Nigeen lake with her husband and their two daughters, Afshan and Nida. The lake in front of her house was lined by a row of colourful houseboats, ensconced by the majestic hills of Zabarwan. Her home was a mini paradise. Aunt Nelofar's temperament and sensibilities complemented her serene surroundings.

I missed her! I asked Mother if I could visit her. She agreed because going to her place was quite easy; I'd board the school bus with my cousins and did not have to depend on Father or Ramzan Kaak to ferry me.

One Thursday afternoon, along with my two younger cousin sisters, I boarded the bus. We reached Aunt Nelofar's place without any hiccups on the way. Upon reaching, we heated the spicy brain curry and had it with tczochvoar. Soon after having the snack, we heard someone walk in through their big, black gate. Back from her college, Aunt Nelofar emerged at the doorway. I was so excited to see her after months that I rushed to hug her. I shouted and showed off that I still remembered the little Persian she had taught me.

'*Aya ba daanish gah rafta boodi?*'

'*Rafta boodam, rafta boodam!*' she replied, and smiled her big, effusive smile as she wrapped her slender arms around me. We hugged each other for a long time. She kissed my forehead and said, '*Loal oasum aamut.*'

I told her that I too had missed her.

We all gathered in their humongous kitchen-cum-living room to have nun chai. As soon as the dusk fell, Aunt Nelofar's mood changed. She turned panicky, her face lost its vigour. She became restless with her eyes transfixed at the gate.

'*Shaam ha gov, tczeir gov*. It's evening already, it's late already,' she kept saying, repeatedly.

That was the first time I had seen my aunt so worried about something so routine. She was waiting for her husband to return from work. I wasn't privy to her anxiety before that evening. In those moments, Aunt Nelofar seemed to be an entirely different person. She looked so fearful and helpless; such a transformation from the confident, knowledgeable, witty and fearless woman I had known.

As soon we heard the engine of her husband's car and saw him walk in, her panic dissipated. I must have been staring at her worriedly because Afshan came close to me and whispered, 'After Papa was kidnapped for three days last year, she gets worried every evening, especially if he gets slightly late.'

I had heard about it at home, but it was for the first time Afshan was telling me about her father's abduction.

'We were at school. Two or three militants had come to ask Papa for donation. He hadn't given any money at that moment.

They asked him for a ride as he was leaving for work. He had to. Within five minutes, they had fished out their guns and taken him with them, leaving the car and the driver behind. For three days, we didn't know where or how he was. There were so many relatives here at home. I don't know who finally helped get him back to us. When he came back home, he said a little girl used to get him food at the hideout. She would remind him of Nida. But Nida doesn't know about any of this. Whenever she asked for Papa, Ammi told her he was in Jammu for work.'

We had an early dinner that night. For a while, Afshan and I played zarab zero (tic-tac-toe) in the dim light. To not have bright lights on, lest we attracted undue attention, had become the norm across the city, the valley. Then, Afshan, Nida and I repaired to their room while Aunt Nelofar and her husband slept in the one adjacent to ours. Both the bedrooms faced the Nigeen lake. Right opposite their house, where the houseboats were parked, stood a small, white, single-storeyed structure: Nigeen Club. It was visible from my aunt's house. Known for its buzzing nightlife in the seventies and the eighties and frequented by tourists from Western countries, it was yet another place occupied by the troops after 1990.

The night was chilly because of the cool breeze emanating from the lake. Afshan and Nida slept on one bed. I slept on a separate one. We faced each other. I insisted on keeping the footlight on. Neither of them agreed. I didn't argue and we dropped off to sleep. Suddenly, in the middle of the night, I was woken by a loud, buzzing sound. I had no clue as to what the strange sound was. I had never heard it before.

'These are motorboats on the lake for night patrol,' Afshan almost whispered.

The sound echoed over the lake.

The aquatic-patrolling troops toured the entire lake, checking for suspected militants and their hideouts. Like that wasn't frightening enough, unusually bright halogen lights were flashed from across the lake from the club. Lights that reached through the windows of my aunt's house and exposed its interiors. The oppressively bright light pierced through the thickest of crewel curtains. It felt like someone held a full moon right in front of our faces.

Afshan and Nida, used to the night patrol perhaps, awoke only once. Nida started sobbing in her sleep. Afshan patted her, almost involuntarily, out of habit. The light shone intermittently. I didn't count the number of times, but I noticed Nida was holding her own neck tightly. Next morning, I learnt that she was wearing a square amulet covered in black cloth.

'She doesn't take it off, not even when she goes to the toilet. I tell her it's a sin to wear amulets to the toilet as they contain holy verses, but she is too scared to go anywhere without it. She thinks if she takes it off, the lights are going to flash again. Before Ammi got her the amulet, she'd cry inconsolably. Sometimes, it looked like she was breaking into a fit when the light was flashed on our house,' Afshan told me.

When I was Nida's age, only darkness scared me, I noted in my head.

During those three nights I stayed at their place, I kept waking up at the slightest beam of light, my heart beating faster than the previous time.

I also kept thinking about my decision to keep the new secret that Afshan had made me privy to. Pulling me aside that morning, she had said, 'Last month, I had gathered a group of girls in the neighbourhood and we all had decided to go to the

UN office at Sonwar with a memorandum. Someone ratted on us and told Ammi. I don't think she has told Abbu yet. He was away for work. But I think he wouldn't mind.

'You know, when he was a student in the 1960s, he and some of his batchmates, along with some foreign journalists, were jailed during a protest in their campus. Maqbool Bhat was in the central jail too! At the same time! Abbu had appeared for his final year engineering exam from the jail.

'But Ammi doesn't understand. She threatened to jump into the lake. I was not allowed to step outside for a few days. Not even to school! But I will gather a more trusted group of friends this time. Why don't you join us too?'

I didn't reply. I don't think she cared for my answer either. She was resolute about her decision of marching to the local UN office.

The following Monday, when Aunt Nelofar packed quince apples and walnuts for Bobeh from her kitchen garden, little did she know that I would also carry back the nocturnal sounds and the flashes of light from her house with me. The memory of the lake patrol didn't let me sleep for many a night. At the slightest murmur, outside or within the house, I would wake up with a start in the dark of the night and struggle to shake off the effects of the epilepsy-inducing flashes of light. I couldn't shake the thought of my aunt's panic-stricken face, Nida's tiny hands holding on to her amulet. Though Afshan boasted of them barely having gone through horrifying crackdowns prevalent everywhere else, she didn't mention how every night their house was searched without anyone entering it physically. I wondered which was worse.

SHARED GRIEF

BOBEH'S JANAZAH WAS GETTING READY to be taken for burial. Father spread a green cloth with Kalima written in golden ink over the coffin. Ajaz Bhaijaan, my cousin sister's husband, came forward. He was the tallest and seemed the strongest amongst all. Maybe his resolute nature came from his having had to carry coffins in the direst situations, I thought. So far, Bobeh's was an ordinary funeral; Bhaijaan had seen extraordinary things happen at funerals, including one where angels from heaven decided to descend to the earth to carry the coffin to the graveyard. Or at least that's what I had imagined had happened to him when he had narrated the event to us and uttered the words, *'Zanneh nyoov jenazeh malaikav vidaan vidaan…'*

That sentence about the flying angels stayed with me ever since I'd heard him describe the fated funeral. That was in May 1990. That year, a new routine had been set. To get out of the bed and rush, half awake, to the spot where the telephone was and mumble two questions into the receiver:

Is the school open today?

Are the buses plying?

If, by some miracle, the phone lines were working, I'd make a call to the school to enquire about it being open. There'd be three scenarios. A 'yes' or a 'no' were simple and direct. The third one upset me the most: 'Yes, the school is open but not all the buses are here.' It meant that some of the buses had ferried children. It also meant that either our area, or some other areas, were on edge that particular morning or had been so since the previous night because of which curfew must have been imposed in select areas. The rest of the city would be unaffected. It upset me immensely. What about the rest of us missing school? Were we so insignificant that our schools could go on without us?

As it was, phoning the school wasn't easy; often, the calls would not go through. So, I'd also try ringing Asiya, one of my classmates who lived a few bus-stops away, closer to the main route. Their line too was busy that day. I alternated between calling Asiya and the school office, frantically. Finally, I got through Asiya's number.

'Hello!'

'Salaam, can I speak to Asiya please?'

'Hi! You know I was about to call you. You heard about Rabia's father?'

'What? Who?'

'He has been killed. Some gunmen shot him dead at their house. Our friend Rabia Farooq. Papa got a call from someone. I'll call you later. He needs to use the phone before it goes dead.'

Rabia was one of our batchmates. Her father, Mirwaiz Maulvi Mohammad Farooq, who also happened to be the chief cleric and a political leader, had been shot dead in his house. Unidentified gunmen had barged into their house at night and showered him with bullets from head to toe. It was one of the many political assassinations by Na-maloom Afraad, differing versions of which came out for years. Some reports said that he was killed by militants for a clash in their ideologies, some said it was the handiwork of the state.

It was his coffin that Ajaz Bhaijaan was one of the pallbearers for. That day, he was one of the survivors of the carnage that the funeral had been turned into.

After that incident at the funeral, Bobeh fell ill. Her asthma worsened. Tear gas, the news! Everything around her made her unwell. Ajaz Bhaijaan visited her one afternoon. He narrated the entire scene to us that day.

After the assassination, the body, instead of being handed over to his family at the hospital, was taken by Maulvi sa'ab's followers and a large procession started towards his ancestral house in Razze Kadal before the burial.

'We started from Sovur. As we passed through Nowshehar, Bagh-e-Ali Mardan Khan, the sea of mourners tripled. People had joined from all the areas. Near Firdaus Cinema, we started chanting "*Jis Kashmir ko khoon se seencha, woh Kashmir humara hai*" loudly. As we inched towards Hawal, we heard gunshots. We were told that CRP had shot down an elderly woman. There was silence for some seconds. No one moved, no one retracted. But we marched on.

'The mourners were chanting the naareh louder. The firing didn't stop. People were being killed and injured. Maulvi sa'ab's coffin shifted from the pallbearers in the front to the pallbearers behind them. The bullets hit the coffin. But we didn't let Maulvi sa'ab fall. I wasn't in the front when we started ... I was somewhere in the middle. I rammed through the crowd when the coffin was seen diving on to the street. It was tough to not stumble on the fallen dead bodies before us. The military had pointed their guns at us the whole time. They kept firing ... I don't know how we managed to carry Maulvi sa'ab amidst all that.'

He ended the description of the horrific incident with the sentence: '*Zanneh nyoov jenazeh malaikav vidaan vidaan.*' Feeling goose pimples appear on my skin, I ended up imagining Rabia's father's coffin flying away.

Two years later, after her father's assassination, Rabia and I happened to walk back to the classroom after recess. We didn't speak about her father, about that summer day when her life changed forever. That was the first time in two years I had walked with her. Just her and me. I wanted to ask her about how she coped with losing him in such a brutal manner. Throughout the walk, I wanted to tell her that one of the young men to shoulder her father's coffin, one who had also braved the bullets had been my cousin's husband, Ajaz Bhaijaan. I wanted to share her grief. But I couldn't talk about it. I didn't have the courage or the words to rake up the past. At that age, silence was the biggest and the only condolence I could offer.

OF MEN, MICE AND VIOLENCE

IN THE MONTHS THAT FOLLOWED, I recreated some of the spaces that Bobeh used to occupy. Her favourite spots were by the windows. I'd tilt the cushions slightly in the corner where she used to sit in the evenings, the way she did whenever she napped. Next to the cushions was her spittoon. On the other side was her prayer rug. I left all of it the way it used to be.

Between performing ablution and praying, Bobeh would sometimes stop by a window, on the west side of our home, which overlooked the courtyard of Naseer's house. My father's thirty-three-year-old cousin, Naseer was commonly called 'doonkalleh' – walnut head – by the neighbourhood kids. Infuriated, he'd chase them away. Naseer had had a fall from the first storey of their house as a child. He had suffered damage in his brain as a result. There was a large bump on the left temple on his largish forehead which had a receding hairline. That made him the subject of ridicule. Able-bodied and handsome in his own way, the only way one could tell there was something not quite right with him was by observing his cognitive skills. Conversations were hardly an issue, but it took him longer to respond to certain tasks, especially if he had been given instructions. He owned a small hosiery and garments shop near Boher Kadal. A genteel and a polite person, he'd occasionally get angry, with outbursts of violence, since he was unable to regulate his emotions.

'Today Naseer was bleeding from the nose again. Some kids teased him and called him doonkalleh near the mosque. He ran after the boys who were faster than him. One of them, oblivious to his condition, pushed him hard to the ground. Naseer fell straight on his face,' said Ramzan Kaak, who kept Bobeh up-to-date about everything untoward that happened to Naseer.

'Takhseer!' Bobeh responded.

Later, she'd tactfully ask after him to his mother, Hajra: 'How's Naseer now? I hope the bleeding has stopped?'

His mother was a woman of simple emotions. In response, she'd always cry inconsolably. 'I have visited all the doctors. I have taken him to all the pirs in the vicinity and in far-flung areas that I hadn't heard of before. Some don't have motorable roads. I ensure that his SOS medication is in the top pocket of his shirt! What use is it? He never remembers to take it, especially during a scuffle. The only way I can die peacefully is when I marry him off. At least, there will be someone to look after him after I am gone. My heart has become weaker,' she'd say, wiping her nose and her moist eyes on the back of the left sleeve of her pheran. 'Thankfully, he is not dependent on anyone when it comes to earning a living.'

Regardless of his condition, Naseer's mother was resolute in her determination to get him married. She didn't have much faith in medicine; she also believed that getting a dutiful and 'shareef' wife would help him change and was his only hope of getting through his life.

Within a few months, in a quiet ceremony, Naseer was married off to Nasreen, a demure woman whose left cheek dimpled when she smiled. She barely spoke or socialized with anyone in the large contingent of relatives that surrounded their house, which included ours. After the wedding, as expected, Nasreen looked after Naseer and helped his mother do the household chores. She was an early riser and often caught Bobeh's eye at the window.

'Naseer is so lucky to have married that girl. Looks like Hajra's prayers have been finally answered,' Bobeh would say to Mother.

To everyone's amazement, Naseer's behaviour did change drastically after the marriage. He appeared less anxious. His susceptibility to engage in fights and the violent outbursts reduced considerably. The relatives attributed the welcome change to Nasreen and her gentle ways of taking care of him. Their lives seemed to be going on smoothly until one unfortunate morning when he forgot his identity card at home.

Naseer had spilled kahwe on his khan dress before leaving for the shop. He had left the identity card in the top left pocket of the shirt he had to take off. As luck would have it, he had to commute that day to replenish his inventory from a slightly far-off wholesale market.

The bus he was travelling on was stopped near a military check post as per routine. The passengers sat still in trepidation, ready with their proofs of existence, their identity cards in their hands. Unable to recall that he had forgotten it at home in his other shirt, Naseer had panicked and fiddled in his pockets and bag to locate his I-card, to no avail. The troops, upon seeing his furtive behaviour, had grown suspicious. They'd hit him a few times with their rifle butts. After a heavy blow, Naseer had fallen unconscious. Luckily, the bus conductor was acquainted with him. He'd seen him take that route often and was kind enough to bring him back to the shop. Naseer took a few days to recover from the blows before he resumed his work at the shop. But that incident had left an indelible mark on him.

A few years later, the devastating news of Nasreen's body being fished out of a river spread like fire on an early morning in the entire neighbourhood. It brought gloom upon all of us.

'He was never normal after the military beat him on the bus. He would wake up in the middle of the night and start beating Nasreen black and blue,' Bibi told Mother.

'Is that why she'd stopped visiting us? She sometimes made gulkand for Bobeh. She said it would help alleviate her cough and asthma,' Mother said.

Bibi divulged that Nasreen, who was reluctant to tell her aged parents about her husband's beatings, would often confide in her. Bibi had seen Nasreen's black eye and a cut lip more than once.

'Who'd believe that Naseer could hit his wife with such bestiality! I sympathized with the poor girl and told her he'd get better with time.' Bibi felt partly guilty that it was the false hope in her advice that had driven Nasreen to desperation and she had taken her own life by jumping into the river.

Naseer was arrested for the abetment of suicide. He was eventually released. As a teenager, the tragedy reminded me of a story about mice, '*Gagar Padshahkath*' that Bobeh often narrated to me when she fed me. It had two endings. Depending on her mood, she'd choose one of them, and each time, I listened to it with the eagerness of the first time because of the unpredictability of the end.

Two mice get married to each other. After they start living together, one day, the buck asks the doe to cook khyeczir for dinner. He buys her all the ingredients and leaves for work. As the doe gets started, she takes a teaspoonful of the mix to taste for seasoning. Then, after adjusting the spices, she tastes a little more to check again for taste and consistency. Pleased with how the porridge has turned out, she gets so carried away that she ends up finishing the entire meal by herself. After it dawns on her that there is hardly anything left for dinner, she panics. She wraps an empty copper bowl in an old blanket and keeps it by the hearth. When the buck returns home, at the end of a hard day, he is excited for the special dinner. Dreading the consequences of her folly, the doe stands away from him and keeps misdirecting him from one place to another.

'Oh, the khyeczir is near the window, next to jajeer. How could I forget where I kept it! I remember now, I left it next to daan, check there.'

Already irked and hungry, when the buck discovers the empty bushkaab, he is livid. He flings the copper lid of the bowl at the doe. It hits her ear, severing it from her head instantly. She bleeds profusely. Amidst pain and panic, she picks up her severed ear and runs out of their house in search of a tailor who can sew it back. Unable to find one at that late hour, she sets out to climb atop a hill and jumps from there.

The other ending that Bobeh would narrate was:

Realizing that he had over-reacted, the buck goes after the doe. He spots her walking up the cliff and runs after her quickly. He apologizes to her. They hug and make up. They climb down the hill together and get her ear fixed. He never lays a finger on her again. They live happily ever after.

I preferred neither ending. I didn't want the doe to be beaten up at all in the first place.

TINY KNOTS OF FAITH

WITHIN MINUTES OF HER COFFIN being taken away, Bobeh was out of sight. Funeral processions before 1989 seemed like a thin trickle. Sometimes, when they would pass by our home, we'd rush to the window in the kitchen and chant '*La Illa ha il lallah*' along with the crowd. Since the 1990s, most funerals of militants or civilians were followed by demonstrations, protests and big marches. People turned out in large numbers. That made the funeral procession of Bobeh look modest despite being made up of nearly a hundred men, including neighbours and relatives, who followed her to the maqbara. Mother, some aunts, cousins and I watched her from the windows of our house as she was being carried away.

I looked at Mother. She didn't seem to notice me. She was immersed in Quranic verses that she had been reciting since the morning and tied a knot at the corner of her dupatta. Mother always covered her head with a dupatta. Not in a conservative way, covering each strand of her hair, but more in the way some Indian actresses back in the sixties and seventies did, her hairline always visible as she'd tuck one side of her dupatta behind her ear, exposing her golden hoop with three garnet roundels dangling from it. She'd let the other side of the opaque fabric flow over her chest, making her long and shapely neck visible. In her youth, she was lovingly called Saira Bano, a popular Hindi film actress, whose aquiline nose and flawless complexion made her look like a quintessential Kashmiri.

Occasionally, Mother tied small knots at the corners of some of her dupattas. If I wore her dupatta during my playtime and untied those knots, she would be furious with me. She'd look hassled each time she saw a crumpled corner from an untied knot. 'Do not ever touch these again without asking my permission,' she reprimanded me one time. Rattled by her disproportionate reaction, I neither apologized nor argued. A couple of times I sulked and vowed to not use her dupatta and instead wear Bobeh's daej, a square-shaped, embroidered bandana, if I had to. But somehow, I'd forget. After being told off a few times, I tried tying the knots again as perfectly as I could, hoping she wouldn't notice. But she could always tell hers apart from mine.

I had noticed Mother tie multiple knots on various occasions. For instance, when my sister Hina went on a date with her fiancé during their courtship. She prayed for my sister to return before Father got home from the shop lest he be upset over her being out that late, chanting Quranic verses while she tied her tiny knots of faith! She also tied them whenever she misplaced some keys or her glasses, so what I failed to fathom was the fuss over the tangled mass of cloth.

It wasn't until an evening in 1991 when I observed her frantically tying the knots again. I keenly watched her, as if it were a performance. It was time for Father to be on his way home from the shop, which was a little over a kilometre from our home. Bobeh, Mother, Koal and I were having nun chai from a small copper samovar when gunshots echoed in the air. '*Yem gai nazdeeke*, that wasn't very far,' Mother said, even as Bobeh panicked. Koal and I continued to sip tea. I fixed my gaze on her.

There was an uproar in the street outside. There had been cross-firing near the bunker at the bridge as people were running for cover. Occasional shrieks of '*Tcza'livo*! Run!' were all that we could hear. There wasn't much time left for the night curfew to be imposed either.

Father got unusually late. He had to take a detour through Fateh Kadal and other by-lanes in the interior parts of the city. That evening, all the four corners of Mother's dupatta were full of knots. She'd helplessly break out into *Ya Shah-i-Hamdan, Ya Rasul Allah, Peer-e-Dastgeer, Ya Hazrat-e-Sultan* aloud, intermittently, invoking as many Sufi saints and prophets as she could remember. She continued her ritual until she heard the main gate open; the thud of its iron handle against the stone wall. Until then, all she did was recite aloud specific Quranic verses, chaar Qul, for his safe return. As soon as she saw him enter the living room, a warm glow suffused her face. She untied the knots upon seeing him.

As I saw her do so, her reprimand reverberated in my head and I realized that the knots were a vault for her personal votive threads, because it was not possible for her to visit a shrine during every crisis. In situations over which she lacked control, in a state of extreme desperation, that was her attempt to seek help of the divine.

Over time, as the number of knots kept increasing, I wondered why she wasn't untying some. Either she was forgetting to do so or there was something else on her mind. Maybe it was the perpetual fear of something happening to Father, hoping that he did not become a victim of an enforced disappearance, praying for him not to be arrested during a crackdown? Maybe it was her secret prayer to keep our house safe from being razed to the ground in a gun-battle? Or was it to keep us all safe from getting killed by bullets? Maybe it was all such fears over which no one had any control…

AFTERLIFE

Q. K.: THE COURTYARD GRAFFITI

MOTHER, MY AUNTS, AND THE rest of the relatives and neighbours went to sit in the drawing room. I didn't join them. I stood where Bobeh used to sit. In her corner of the living room, by the window. It overlooked our courtyard and the narrow 'wall of resistance', as I had started calling it in my head. It was a cemented portion of the brick wall around the house of Father's cousin.

In the autumn of 1990, Ammaji was petrified of two letters.

'The military is going to kill us all when they read what he writes on the wall. I shiver with fear,' Ammaji told Bobeh, in a grave tone accompanied by sobs.

'*Khoda karih sahlei,*' Bobeh responded to her, rather inexpressively, perhaps untrusting of her own words of assurance. As soon as Ammaji was out of earshot, Bobeh would lament Riyaz's scribbling on the walls of their house. Each time she saw Riyaz near the wall, she'd comment, '*Log ye beyyi kaaras. Moaj maryes.* There he goes again. His mother will die of fear.'

Riyaz's mother, Ammaji, as we'd call her, was known for her animated expressions and a strong downtown Srinagar accent, always drawling the last word of her sentences.

Riyaz's wall scribbles were visible from our living room, especially from where Bobeh used to sit. Their house was to the north of ours. Our courtyards were divided by a short wall which was painted with turquoise livun.

Riyaz was the son of my father's cousin. He was around twenty-three years of age, same as my sister Hina. A recluse by nature, when the boys his age would loiter about town, ogling at women or discussing politics on Waan Pyenj in the evenings, he'd be reading books, and filling up the wall and his time with different styles and sizes of two letters:

Q. K., Q. K., Q. K., q. k., Q. K., q. k., q. k., Q. K.

That was much before I had seen 'GO INDIA GO', 'Al-Umar', '*Taejub hai aap ko namaz ke liye fursat nahin*' graffiti appear on the walls of schools, colleges, cinemas or on the shutters of the shops which remained shut most of the time. The one Riyaz used to inscribe on the wall of their house was nothing like that.

No embellishments, no outlines. 'Q.K.' in as many fonts and sizes as he managed to mark with a piece of charcoal. Given that coal was abundant in our storage, as fuel for kanger in winter, procuring it in any season was never a problem.

Riyaz's letters bothered not only Ammaji, but I too was equally tormented by them.

In 1988, he had started scribbling them occasionally. It made me curious to know what they stood for. For a long time, I assumed that maybe those two letters were the initials or nicknames he and his beloved had given to each other. I tried to unravel the mysterious 'Q.K.' in my own ways. I hopped across to our courtyard, and in a stealthy corner, I'd imitate his writing, as if by trying that the riddle would somehow unravel by itself. Sometimes, I read it as 'Qaaf Keef', from right to left, like we did in Urdu.

Like a detective, I started to observe Riyaz keenly whenever he and his friends invited me to play cricket with them in the courtyard. I occasionally bowled for them and was miserable at it. I fielded, and being the youngest, my job was essentially to fetch the ball from odd crevices. We played during civil curfew, which weren't as dreadful as the curfew itself.

Even during our games, Riyaz remained shrouded in mystery. While most of us retorted to a simple cricket jargon, 'Howzat!' to exclaim or appeal, that we had learnt from the commentators on radio and television, Riyaz would exclaim, 'By Clive!'

The Clive mystery was solved in the spring of 1992. Pakistan had won the Cricket World Cup against Australia. Soon after, Hina and I had a telephonic conversation.

'Will Riyaz Bhaijaan say "By Imran" now?'

'I really doubt that. Imran Khan didn't win against India. For him it will always be Clive Lloyd, the captain of West Indies' cricket team who beat India in Kashmir! Can you imagine the courage of the youths who took to the ground and dug the pitch to protest the holding of that match? He wishes he were a part of the crowd that had cheered for West Indies and booed the Indian players. I keep telling him he could have been arrested for pitch digging too. But it won't be for Imran Khan, you see.'

After the 1992 Cricket World Cup, Riyaz became more explicit in his expression and elaborated Q.K. too. He never went back to the acronym but repeatedly wrote the full form on that wall of their house. His mother, Ammaji, kept erasing the words with rags, mops, her dupatta, fearing the wrath of the troops. She'd erase. He'd write. She'd erase again. He'd write in larger and more prominent letters, which left visible traces no matter how hard Ammaji tried to rub it clean. Nothing deterred Riyaz. The entire wall was filled with two words and their shadows: 'Quit Kashmir'.

THE SAINTLESS

FROM THE WINDOW, I SAW an unfamiliar face walk through the courtyard. She was wearing a maroon pheran that I instantly recognized. It had belonged to Bobeh. Suddenly, I remembered that I had seen her a while back. She was the professional funeral bather. Customarily, she had to be given some of the deceased's clothing. Mother had sent for Rajje Maas, but there was no sign of her arrival.

Rajje Maas used to live nearby. She used to address Bobeh as 'moaj' – mother. She visited us at least once a week and whenever she did, she'd light up the living room with her anecdotes. She used to call me Tobruk, because one of the wishes that was granted by praying at the shrine of Baba Reshi, a Sufi saint, included me. I missed hearing that story because she stopped visiting us. I now realized how I would never be able to hear Bobeh narrate the story of the miracle that had been witnessed by the followers and the passers-by at the Sufi shrine of Sheikh Hamza, also known as Makhdoom saeb.

'Many years ago, there was a middle-aged woman, who experienced an excruciating pain in her right ear. It went on for months. She had been to all the doctors in her village and the nearby villages. She decided to try doctors in the city, but it seemed like no one had any cure for her pain. Having given up on modern-day medicine, she went to seek the blessings of Makhdoom saeb and to pray to be cured of the malaise.

'Reaching the shrine, situated near the summit of Koh-i-Maran hill, was not easy since one had to climb over one hundred steps. Before embarking on the steep hike to reach the aastaan, the woman decided to rest awhile. She purchased a small container of warm milk, and tczochvoar from a nearby shop. After she finished the milk and bread, she placed the warm earthen pot that she'd drunk milk from under her head, making up for the absence of a proper pillow.

'After close to half an hour, when she woke up from her nap, she felt an unusual relief in her right ear. The throbbing was gone; she felt no pain! Then, she discovered that the pot of milk under her head was infested with hundreds of centipedes … The insects had fallen from the inside of her ear due to fermentation.

She screamed and sobbed, screamed and sobbed. A large crowd gathered around her. Everyone called it a miracle cure that could only be achieved at the doorstep of the shrine of Makhdoom saeb.'

Bobeh often narrated this story with the same consistency of awe to express her reverence. '*Peer ni boad, yakeen thodh,* faith is as potent as the saint,' she'd say. It was her way of ensuring that I too developed etiqaad in the saints and visited the aastaan regularly. 'Such is the mojeza that a Sufi saint is capable of,' she'd have a furrow on her right eyebrow as she'd say that. To pass on her beliefs, she'd narrate the many miracles performed by all the Sufi masters.

Rajje maas used to narrate a similar story that I'd never get bored of hearing. It was the story about how I was conceived.

'Before you came into this world, your mother suffered a miscarriage. Another pregnancy had been ruled out by the doctors. It devastated her, naturally. She hardly ate anything for days and slept for long hours. She didn't cook. At times, she forgot to pray. That is when I pleaded with her that she should visit the aastaan of Baba Reshi, near Tangmarg.'

The enormous Rajje Maas was perhaps the staunchest believer of the saint in all of downtown Srinagar. She had three daughters and had desperately wanted a son for several years. So, she visited Baba Reshi's shrine a few times and prayed in earnest, until she became pregnant with her fourth child, who turned out to be a boy. Javed was not just her darling son, the cynosure of her eyes, but also a testimony to her Etiqaad.

Traditionally, couples who wanted a male child prayed at the shrine, but Rajje Maas was convinced that if my mother prayed there with all her heart, she, too, would be blessed with a child, regardless of the gender. Mother, who saw no hope in bearing a child again, jumped at anything that came with the slightest promise of the possibility of another pregnancy. She had shown utmost alacrity at undertaking it. Mother made umpteen trips to the shrine until her wish was granted.

'Only a few months afterwards, your mother was blessed with a pregnancy. *Navi reyt zaayakh tczi*, you were born nine months later.'

Bobeh always smiled effusively at that point in the story. Each time Rajje Maas visited our home, she'd call me *Resh sund Tobruk*. I'd remember her soundless laughter that accompanied that sentence, until she stopped laughing altogether. It was in the winter of 1991. Javed, her only son, who had just turned sixteen, was arrested during one of the nocturnal raids in the neighbourhood.

Rajje Maas had run after the speeding vehicle. She had begged the officers to let go of her son, who was yet to finish high school. She had run after the jeep until it had faded from her sight along with her son. She spent months, which turned into years, visiting most of the prisons across the valley looking for Javed. She travelled to jails in Jammu and Udhampur. Some officials had told her that a large number of prisoners had been shifted there. Once, she was offered money by the officials to withdraw the case.

'I have to know where they have kept him. If he is dead, why don't they return his body to me so that I can bury him with my own hands? Where am I going to find him? There is no graveyard that I haven't visited looking for him. When I was yet to conceive him, he made me run from one shrine to another. Where will I look for him now? Which saint will help me find my Javed?'

Every single time she said that, she'd break down. But she was determined to find her son, dead or alive. She stopped bothering about the marriages of her daughters, something that used to occupy her all the time before Javed's disappearance.

One spring afternoon, she visited our house after a long time. It was a year before Bobeh died and we were all glad to see her. She sounded somewhat optimistic as she drank nun chai and declared between her sips to Mother, 'I will go to Baba Reshi's shrine and pray there for Javed's return.'

She didn't step out of her house much after that. She rarely visited us. She neither visited the shrine again, nor did Javed return. She didn't turn up for Bobeh's funeral either.

THE ATTIC AND THE SIEVE

I HADN'T GONE UP TO the attic in months. None of us did unless it was urgent. From the nineties onwards, it was a space best avoided. But that day, going there was unavoidable. I needed more winter wear. With relatives dropping in for condolences, and the house being packed most of the day, I was not being able to sit and study in peace. Mother and Father decided that I should stay at Hina's for a few days. Therefore, I needed more cardigans and a woollen scarf to wear to the freezing exam venue. All our extra woollens were stored inside the trunks that had been shifted to the attic to make room for guests.

At one point, the attic used to be the most frequented part of our tall house. It served many purposes. The last time I had visited it was to perform a ritual for my left eye that was swollen from a nasty stye. Bobeh suggested that I warm some cotton on the iron and apply warm compress. I tried that and it provided temporary relief, but the smarting and the pain persisted. As the days progressed, self-medication proved ineffective too. Neosporin, despite its regular application over two days, thrice a day, didn't work either. The best option was to visit the clinic of the family ophthalmologist, if only that was feasible. The clinic of the ophthalmologist was in Maisuma Bazar, the area that some newspapers called the 'Gaza Strip of Kashmir'. It would be nothing short of a miracle to find his clinic open.

Stuck at home with pain and discomfort, I started to wonder if I could somehow exchange the stye with some other manageable illness. I wished it could magically transform into zaal, chilblains, instead. It was easier to find a home remedy for chilblains, than it was for stye. Chilblains, a common cold sore that most Kashmiris are prone to contracting in winter, finds its cure in the season that it's most prevalent in. All we'd need was the winter necessity – kanger – which every Kashmiri guards close to themselves during the bitterly cold months. We had to simply rinse the hand that we ate with, after dinner, in the plate that we had eaten in. A hot coal was grabbed from the kanger, dipped in the same water before the heat of the ember died down. Then, it was dabbed lightly on the blains. Known to work instantly, the affected area would start itching, which was the first sign of recovery. Done repeatedly for a couple of nights, the sore dried and the crust fell off leaving a light pink scar that would disappear in a week's time.

However, Bobeh believed that the stye too could be cured through an ancient rite, but that required visiting the attic. Waking up before sunrise, I had to carry a sieve to the topmost floor of the house and look at the rising sun through it. The same action was to be performed for three consecutive days. The important condition, according to Bobeh, was that I had to stare at the sun through the sieve without blinking, for a whole minute. Our house, being the tallest one in the neighbourhood, with the least obstructions in the way, served as a perfect place for doing the ritual.

In fact, before the 1990s, each time there was a marriage procession in the neighbourhood, the attic would act as the vantage point for us from which to watch it uninterrupted. Mother didn't frequent the shrine of Shah Hamdan as regularly as Father did, but each time she felt like saying a prayer, she'd climbed up the stairs to the attic too. She would face the shrine to make a wish or say a prayer. There were times when she, at the same spot, cried inconsolably as she watched the processions commemorating the martyrdom of Imam Hussain and his six-month-old son Ali Asghar during Muharram, before such gatherings were banned by the state. On some days, she gazed peacefully at the tomb, the magnificent piece of architecture that one of the rulers of Kashmir, Budshah Zain-ul-Abideen, had built for his mother.

Besides being our watchtower, the attic was a relaxing site for me because it had an unobstructed view of the sky. For Father, it was the possession of pride. He was the proud owner of 'the tallest house in the neighbourhood'. It was one of the few houses in the congested neighbourhood of downtown Srinagar that could be approached from all the four sides: through the main gate, then via the two side-doors from the courtyard side, which further opened into the courtyards of Father's cousins, and the fourth access was through the main street. It also meant our house could never be a hideout for militants nor could we host them for lunches or dinners as was prevalent in the rest of the neighbourhood. Most often, the aides intimated the head of a house about a surprise lunch or dinner that they had to cook for a group of militants. They always chose houses which had escape routes that merged into other houses or into alleyways in case there was a crackdown or a raid. But then, quickly enough, our house became the source of perpetual trepidation of another kind. The very cause of our pride became the cause of worry: the height of the house. The top part, especially the attic, attracted bullets as the cliché 'sweets attract flies' goes. In a matter of a few months, the attic was barely recognizable and became inaccessible to us. None of us ventured upstairs unless necessary. Being closer to the ground was safer. It meant one could duck, hide, lie on the ground. Dodging bullets was easier. Inside the house, the topmost floor became the most dangerous. The wall on the outside of the attic became pockmarked as the clay on the bricks flaked off from stray bullets. It was as if a giant sieve was spread all over it.

SOUNDS AND THE SILENCER

IT WAS TWO DAYS AFTER the funeral. I was trying to prepare for my exam and babysit my sister Hina's two-year-old son, Moosa, at the same time. I hummed some songs into his ear that put him to sleep. Bobeh used to do that too; that, and dab some holy water on his forehead. The same way Mother used to dab some on Hina's belly when she was pregnant with Moosa after she had witnessed the aftermath of a shootout.

Hina got pregnant a year after her wedding – a piece of news that brought us all immense joy. Mother refrained from telling the relatives until Hina's baby bump was amply visible. Father's reaction was largely muted. Bobeh opened her old trunks and dug out tiny woollens with matching woollen caps that my aunts had knitted for me. I didn't care much about the gender of the baby. What excited me was when we shopped for little, minuscule things, pretty clothing and tiny shoes. I thought I would finally get to throw my weight around with someone younger to me in the family.

After the initial few months, Mother frequently visited Hina's house. She didn't dare to bring her over to downtown Srinagar, Shehr-e-Khaas, especially during her last trimester. Once, one of our neighbour's daughters, Ruhi, went into labour in the early hours of a morning before the night curfew was lifted. Even with the valid curfew passes and a visibly pregnant woman in the car, they were stopped at multiple checkpoints by the troops, asked to provide unnecessary details. Obviously, that caused a delay and added to Ruhi's labour pain. They couldn't make it to the maternity ward in time. She had to deliver her baby in the corridor of the hospital. Mother procured holy water through Bibi for Hina to shield her from a situation like Ruhi's.

Mother's visits to Hina's house were paced at regular intervals. She visited once in two weeks interspersed with daily phone calls. Towards the due date, she'd send Ramzan Kaak every Sunday to call on her. It was an unusual practice to let a woman deliver her first child at her husband's house. Usually, women stay at their mothers' homes for at least two months leading up to the due date. But here, the dilemma for Father and Mother was whether to keep a tradition alive or risk two lives. The sustained anticipation for months on end of good news was a new thing for us, especially in times when death and misery had dominated every other house in the valley. We tried to contain the excitement. Mother always warned that anything overdone, in excess, had the potential to quickly turn into its opposite. When Hina and I used to sometimes break into a bout of hysterical, unending laughter, she instructed us to look at our fingernails (*naman kun vuchev*). According to her, that was the easiest way to distract us and bring an abrupt end to the laughter, lest it brought some misery upon us.

To make up for not being able to look after my sister the way she'd have liked to, Mother always accompanied Hina to the routine visits to her gynaecologist. During one such visit, I insisted that I join them too. Soon it turned to be a family outing as Father offered to drive us to her place to pick her up, go to the clinic and drive back together.

The day was going as per the plan which was a big thing in itself: not being delayed by detours, cross-firing, abrupt encounters. We picked Hina up from her in-laws' before driving to the clinic. The wait there wasn't too long. Before dropping her back, Mother told Father that she needed to buy some dry fruits and assorted snacks for Hina who had developed gestational diabetes. She needed to nibble at regular intervals. It was around three o'clock. We had enough time to see her off and drive back before the imposition of the night curfew around six. Father drove towards Residency Road to the grocer. Mother, Hina and I alighted outside the grocery store. Father didn't join us but instead drove off to see a friend of his who owned a business outlet nearby. He promised to return soon to fetch us.

The store had several shelves filled with imported ingredients for baking and cooking. Other than spices and tea packs, it had large containers of branded orange juice that Father had brought with him when he'd gone for Hajj a few years ago. Mother chose a mix of almonds, walnuts, apricots, cashew nuts, pistachios and raisins.

Holding on to a hot water bottle, Hina sat on a stool next to the staircase that led to the gallery full of excess supplies. With her swollen feet and protruding belly under the layers of winter clothing, and an oversized pheran with a large patch of tilleh in the shape of a Chinar leaf, she looked thrice her usual size. She seemed slightly tired but in a good mood. Haji sa'ab, the kind grocer, gave us a handful of almonds and dried apricots that she started munching on.

Even though it was only around four, it was already dark. Mother was paying the bill; a salesman was packing her things. Meanwhile, she kept glancing outside. 'It's getting late, where's your father?' She wore a worrisome expression on her face, her eyebrows knitted together. She made the payment and waited for a while. As time passed slowly, the restlessness within her grew. She moved the bags aside on the counter and asked me to stay guard to my sister. 'I'll go fetch your father.'

Barely five minutes into her stepping out, armoured vehicles and paramilitary personnel sprang out of nowhere. They spread like a synapse on the street. The large vehicles cast darker shadows inside the shop, making it look like a dreary night.

People hurriedly dispersed in various directions as the troops took their positions. The shutters of the shops came down one after another in no time, making loud and ominous sounds. Haji sa'ab, the grocer, despite the risk to his shop and staff, did not pull the shutters down completely because he could see my sister Hina had turned all crimson. She looked even more swollen. He tried to console her, but instead of being pacified, she started crying. 'Mamma, Papa,' she went on and on and on like an inconsolable child.

Standing next to the counter, Hina then began trembling. I was pleading with her to sit down but she kept shifting her weight from one leg to another while leaning against the counter, sobbing. Instead of offering more comforting words, a sudden gush of resolve came over me and I told her that I'd go and fetch Mother and Father. She didn't react and continued crying.

Outside, I learnt that there had been a shootout in the area where the shop of Father's friend was situated. A plainclothes policeman was shot at point-blank range. Two militants riding on a scooter had stopped right next to him and shot him, killing him instantly. They had had a pistol with a silencer. That's why nobody had heard the gunshots as the man had crumbled to the ground dissolving into a pool of his own blood.

I walked to the road that led to the site of the shootout. I saw Father's empty car parked opposite the shooting spot. There were no civilians on the road. I was the only person. The only girl. Somehow, I couldn't go further. I turned back, my thoughts astray and incoherent.

Where was Father? Hopefully at his friend's shop? Was that shut? Maybe Mother was with him too? It was odd. I couldn't remember anything that I had seen ten seconds ago. I was trying to recall if what I had just seen on the streets was blood or a body lying in blood. A black, dense fog came over me, wiping out the details of the scene, involuntarily.

'What if the troops stop me, what should I tell them? Would they ask me why I was walking alone? Why weren't they shooting me already?' With those thoughts, I bent to enter the grocer's half-shut shop the shutters outside which had been lowered further. Hina seemed in a semi-conscious state. I rubbed her hands. She didn't ask me anything, either about Father or about Mother. We waited for almost an hour, maybe less, but whatever time passed, it felt like eternity.

The siege was lifted, the army vehicles drove off. The clouds had cleared, the evening was bright again. Father arrived outside the grocer's in his car. I helped Hina get inside it.

'Where is Mother? She went to fetch you?' I asked Father.

Seeing Hina's pale face, her pregnancy glow turned ashen, he remained quiet. He turned the car around and started driving back to the site of the shootout. Midway, we spotted Mother looking dishevelled, walking towards the direction of the grocery store. She was making a peculiar movement with her hand, a gesture which indicated uncertainty or refusal, as if she was saying no to something. She'd mumble something under her breath and oscillate her bony right hand. After that incident, every time she panicked, making that hand gesture became a habit for her.

'*Zuv hai vandai,*' Mother held Hina's face in her cupped palms as she uttered those words of endearment. Hina closed her eyes. For a second, I thought she had passed out.

When we went to drop my sister at her home, she insisted that Mother stayed with her that night. Father and I drove back with the lights of the car switched on inside, complying with the military diktat, since it had already started to turn dark.

A month and a half later, Mother's wish was granted, and Hina gave birth to my nephew Moosa. A beautiful baby boy; his head full of soft and fluffy curls. He had an angelic face. His hazel eyes made him look like a smaller version of our grandfather. Otherwise a healthy child, as he grew older, he turned out to be petrified of sounds. He'd cry bitterly if someone shut the door loudly.

That afternoon after Bobeh's funeral, as I was preparing for my exam, Hina's mother-in-law called me for lunch and I responded to her a little too loudly. Their kitchen was adjacent to the living room where I was sitting. Next to me, Moosa had just woken up from his nap. At my loud 'Haeev', he shrieked and jumped into my lap, trembling. He held my pheran with his tiny hands as tightly as he could. He couldn't be consoled until he fell asleep again. I thought he was missing Hina who was away, helping our Mother with preparations for a prayer ceremony for Bobeh, which was to be held the following day. As I watched my little nephew sleep, a thought came over me. I suddenly wondered if his fears had anything to do with the chaos and trauma that he must have absorbed in Hina's belly on the day of the shootout near the grocer's shop when she and I had presumed our parents to have been killed.

GAMES OUR CHILDREN PLAY

OMAR KIDNAPPED AHMAD. THEY WERE brothers.

'*Yi rozze hameshe' khocze' be'd*. He will always be a coward … Had it been us, we'd have kicked the bellies of the kidnappers. How can you not recognize the touch of a twig from that of the barrel of a gun?'

When Omar played a prank on Ahmad, it had a lot to do with the years they were born in. Ahmad was born in the early eighties and Omar was born later in that decade. The lived next to Hina's house. While studying, I had heard laughter and shrieks and had looked out. It was then that Omar, the younger brother, narrated the entire incident to me from their porch as I watched intently from the windowsill.

'Ahmad, the big doctor he is planning to be, was returning from private tuitions. As soon as he left the tuition centre, my friends Zafar, Faisal and I followed him with our faces masked. He either goes to school or comes back home. He is so boring, follows the same habits like a robot. But he is a fast walker, as if already late to reach somewhere important!'

Omar then enacted how the boys quickened their pace to match Ahmad's hurried steps. 'Then Zafar poked him with a twig on his left shoulder blade and our dear Ahmad assumed it was a gun! So, next, Faisal blindfolded him. In the meanwhile, I had stopped an autorickshaw. Then, we threatened him, asking him to obey us, or else he would be "responsible for the consequences"! Our dear Ahmad had obviously no choice then but to do as he was told. We bundled Ahmad into the rickshaw!'

Omar paused to guffaw. Then he continued: 'I sat next to the driver and gestured at him to halt after going some way. I'm sure, by then Ahmad's knees had turned into a wobbly mess. Zafar, still poking Ahmad's back with the pointy twig, "the gun", asked him to get out of the vehicle and walk ahead. Ahmad was sure that those would be the last steps of his life. Then, after we all had walked a bit, Faisal undid his blindfold. He looked like a corpse! Pale, stunned! Staring at me. Yes, it was me, his dear little brother, in front of him. We had taken our kerchief masks off.'

Omar paused again to laugh hysterically. 'Can you believe that? He's so stupid. A proper coward! So much so, after all we did to him, he didn't even curse us properly.'

As I listened to him, Hina had come in with Moosa and tea. She had heard most of Omar's story. After I shut the window, she sighed and observed, 'I wonder if kids born in the pre-Tehreek era are unlike those born in the post-Tehreek era. Perhaps that explains the difference in their pranks...'

'How do you mean?'

'Well, to me, the former seem to be more fearful, contemplative and ... distressed. Of course, children born in the post-Tehreek era too could be contemplative and distressed, but what distinguishes them from the ones born before the active resistance movement is the lack of fear! That, and this envious ability to laugh at fear in its face, exactly like Omar and his friends. Something I could never imagine the pre-Tehreek children like Ahmad or us do,' she said.

I wanted to tell her that my hair-pulling had intensified after Dr Rubaiya Sayeed was kidnapped. Perhaps Ahmad's reaction was delayed, which made his brother mock at him. Perhaps Ahmad was thinking of vice chancellor Mushir-ul-Haq's kidnapping and killing? With that thought, I realized that the old games that we played before 1989 had long disappeared from the streets, from our courtyards. Traces of coal markings, drawn to make hopscotch, that would be seen in every neighbourhood, and common and private courtyards, could hardly spotted anymore because by the time it was the play hour, evening curfew would be imposed. Evenings, which used to be full of screams and squeals of children playing chuppan-chuppai, hide-and-seek, or lakad-lakad, were now heavy and full of lull. These days, it was common to see children enact scenes of an 'encounter' between the troops and the militants or be busy making toy guns out of wooden planks and discarded wires. I wondered which games my nephew and his friends would pick when they grew up.

THE DREAD OF DASTARKHWAAN

'ARE YOU ON A DIET?'

Hina's mother-in-law asked me at lunch after I refused to eat most of the dishes laid out on dastarkhwaan. There was a non-vegetarian dish of aloo-bukhara chicken, and a vegetarian one called tczaek waangan. Food had once again started tasting the same as it did at home, except for the vegetable dish, because they had made it with dried brinjals from hokhsyun: the winter vegetable repertoire.

Hokhsyun, the dried vegetables, are prepared in summer. A staple food for most of us in winter, the dried vegetable fibre has a distinct taste.

In our household, preparing hokhsyun was an elaborate affair. In summer, Ramzan Kaak would bring home a wicker basket full of tomatoes, bottle gourd and aubergine. Mother would clean and dice them. Meanwhile, Bobeh would prepare reams of thick, white thread bought specially for stringing the vegetables. She'd pierce the diced vegetables with a thick needle used to embroider namda rugs and string them into garlands. Next, she'd hand the garlands over to Ramzan Kaak, who would hang them outside, from the many windows of the first floor. The vegetables were left out to dry in the sun for days on end until their outer rims crinkled and became crisp. Much later, they were unstrung and stored away in gunny sacks. Hokhsyun ensured that we always had ample food to eat. It was a necessity in the cold months because, for most parts of it, road links between Kashmir and India would be cut off. Large trucks carrying poultry and other food supplies grown in the plains would get stuck on the precarious highway.

I have largely been a fussy eater, but that day, I didn't know how to explain it to my sister's mother-in-law. My fussiness had a lot to do with a habit I had picked up from Father. He often complained about Mother's cooking, his primary grouse being about the visible rim of excess oil in the curries she made. Whatever the dish – succulent roundels of turnip with mutton or diced bottle gourd in a mint-and-yoghurt paste – he carefully gathered all the surrounding oil on a ladle and presented it before Mother, grinning sheepishly.

'Have bad days fallen on us, *Khoda raechin*? All my relatives use more oil than I do. Even my late mother did. It means something. It says something about us. That we are not nouveau riche but have old money. Should we not eat the way we deserve to?' was Mother's oft-repeated response.

'Must our khandaan's reputation depend on oil? That'll be slippery. It would taste as good with less oil,' would be Father's retort.

Sometimes they squabbled about it. But most days, Mother ignored Father's comments or dismissed them as his limitation, not being able to understand her affluent background. For me, their dinner-table bickering was an introduction to love – little quarrels which either dissipated on their own, or after an effort, in private. Maybe after everyone else had gone off to sleep, Father mollified her with romantic couplets or gifted her trinkets the next day. Perhaps that is how they kept the romance in their relationship alive: by bickering in front of others and making up when alone.

Since the winter of 1990, Mother started adding excess water to curries to make each dish last longer. I couldn't reconcile with the fact that she had adjusted to using less oil and more water in her cooking. I didn't think that would ever be possible. Mother was someone who took pride in her extravagant recipes; she was known for cooking fish elaborately, over three days. Even when cooking our regular meals, she liked the meat and vegetables to be marinated in spices so rich that the entire house would be suffused with the distinct aroma of her cooking. But after 1990, like so many aspects of our lives, Mother's kitchen too seemed unfamiliar. The way food tasted changed. Father and Mother bickered less at the dastarkhwaan. I detested the new kind of watery curries. Besides, over the years, the smells of certain foods were associated with different incidents which I didn't want to remember.

In 1993, for example, for four consecutive months, Mother had noticed something I had not, though it concerned me! 'You hardly eat these days, you look so thin,' Mother told me in an accusatory tone, one day. 'After two morsels you don't touch a single grain on the plate. Are you dieting?'

'NO!'

'Then why this allergy towards food?'

I didn't know how to explain to her that I wasn't doing it on purpose. Eating exasperated me. My aversion didn't only have its root in the way food tasted, but also in how it looked and smelt.

Each time Mother cooked potatoes-and-lamb, which had become our curfew meal, I cringed. The dish no longer had the warmth and comfort it had when it was cooked on the days when there was no curfew. Would Mother take offence if I told her that the curries were watery and insipid? I didn't dare to. I also stayed away from my favourite bread, tczochvoar, as much as I could. Earlier, the aroma of freshly baked bread coming out of the bakery with green paint, at the corner of the street, always worked up my appetite. It wouldn't matter if I had had a meal just before – the whiff of a fresh bread being pulled out of a hot tandoor passing our window was an impulse that I had to always act on. In summer, I'd grab a large piece of the bread and have it with yoghurt. In winter, I'd generously slather butter over it and gulp down two big ones with nun chai. Since the routine evening patrol by the troops started in 1990, the aroma of the bread blended with the sound of jackboots. Bite, boots. It made my appetite disappear.

On the eve of Eid in 1989, when I was mistaken to be my slain cousin who was the same age as me, the entire house was steeped in the aroma of palak kokur – spinach and chicken. Thereafter, every time Mother cooked that dish, the smell made me instantly nauseous. Palak kokur started smelling of death, but I didn't know how to make Mother understand.

She insisted I visit Saleema. '*Tcze tchai naaf dejmicz.* Your solar plexus is malfunctioning.'

Usually, twice every year, in winter and summer, mostly during the school vacations, regardless of my appetite, Mother would take me to Saleema. The thought of Saleema's toe made me squirm.

Saleema had been known to our family for a long time. Much before I was born, she used to come to our place to sell fish. After losing her left leg in an accident, Saleema was largely confined to the two-room house that she and her much younger brother used to live in. Known to possess immense curative powers, she had most of the womenfolk from the neighbourhood frequent her. Saleema appeared in Mother's head before a doctor did each time she felt nauseous, lethargic or suffered a loss of appetite.

Saleema believed that the right alignment of the energy centre in one's body largely led to our well-being. She seemed to have mastered the ways to correct the misaligned bunch of nerves. She'd practise the same ritual over three days. She'd start by massaging the tummy with warmed up mustard oil, from all the sides, gathering 'the energy' just above the navel. Then, she'd seal this energy: first, by applying pressure through the tip of a knife that she'd placed on the belly button, and then, by pinning the energy down with her big toe. All the while, she would recite Quranic verses under her breath. The last act was the toughest part – her crusty big toe on my navel! Sometimes it was ticklish, but mostly it felt like Saleema dug a large nail right into the pit of my stomach. The ritual was carried out preferably before lunch. After reaching home, Mother fed me hot, steaming rice with haakh, collard greens, cooked with garlic and green chillies. Surprisingly, after three days of going through this nightmare, my digestion did improve. It seemed to work until the next cycle of kamzooriy, loss of appetite and occasional lethargy, kicked in.

Thinking it to be a case of misalignment in my solar plexus again, Mother dragged me to Saleema's, but to no avail. This time around, not much changed after the energizing ritual. Instead, as the years went by, the distance between food and me increased. It was beyond Saleema's powers to erase the associations that I had developed with mealtimes. She could do nothing. And I couldn't help but eat less.

THE ATTESTED DEAD

THE TWO BABY POTATOES ROASTING in my kanger were making crackling sounds as I picked up the newspaper from the previous day. I paused at the obituary section. It read: 'Rasm-e-Chaharum. 22 December 1994. Sarwa Begum. Ahlia, Maqbool Shah.'

The words appeared blurry as warm tears welled up in my eyes for the first time since Bobeh had died. I didn't want to cry with Hina's in-laws around and so, I concentrated hard on rest of the sections in the newspaper the way I would on any other day.

Routinely, I browsed the job vacancies section in the newspaper first. I would read with great interest the details that appeared alongside calls for engineering contracts and tenders, jobs in government sectors, walk-in interviews at unaffiliated computer centres and teaching posts in public schools. Going through the advertisements always made me wonder which one I would be eligible for only a few years later, after graduating from college. Even though I was yet to graduate from high school, the aspect of a future job that brought the promise of being independent in a few years' time was an intoxicating thought.

At Hina's house, no one seemed to be in a rush to read the newspaper. In ours, grabbing the papers was a daily struggle. We would receive the Urdu newspaper first. Father would go through it cursorily in the mornings. He carried it to the shop to fill in the dull periods of the day with as much reading as he could manage. In the evenings, the English daily arrived from Delhi at the shop, for which he reserved two hours of his time after dinner. Not that they'd carry much news, or accurate news from the valley, but Father liked to keep abreast of current world affairs. Sometimes, he commented on the stark difference of what was really happening in Kashmir and how differently it was being presented to the world outside.

'A territorial dispute sold as the rock-bed of terrorism!' He pointed out such differences but also advised me, 'You should read the editorial section, it's usually well-written.'

1990 onwards, the English daily hardly arrived in time or regularly because of perpetual curfew and hartal. The honest man that he was, our newspaper vendor brought home a stack of all the ones that we had not received on the day that he could finally step out for deliveries again.

As the number of days under curfew increased and shops were mostly shut, Father was forced to stay at home. He'd read the Urdu daily from end to end, for hours. When he napped in the afternoon and the newspapers would be lying around, it would be our turn to get a hold of it. Six sheets of unpalatable happenings!

Headlines and numbers, ordinary people turned into statistics.

Das afraad halaaq, bees loag jaan bahaq – ten people killed, twenty dead. Statistics! Statistics! Mass killings, firing on unarmed protestors, grenade blasts killing civilians and troops. More statistics!

Shehri
Fauji
Shehri, shehri, shehri, shehri
Fauji
Jung joo
Shehri, shehri
Jung joo
Fauji
Jung joo
Shehri, shehri
Jung joo

Halaaq!

All those horrific headlines were punctuated with photographs of men with disfigured faces and gaping mouths.

Occasionally, a big, smudged blot of ink appeared in the place of an eye which probably was dried blood in a hollow socket. Thank God for the black-and-white newspapers where blood appeared grey. Most of the times, the bodies were made to pose in the same way: in a line, as if the dead were on display. It seemed like a warning, a cautionary tale about the fate of anyone who would dare to fight for the right to self-determination. In some photographs, the bodies of militants had mounds of bullets along with guns – AK-47, Rocket launchers – by their sides or in the background. All of it looked like a coveted prize, a trophy. The dead militants looked helpless, yet powerful at the same time. 'The will of these youth to take on a well-trained army of over 600,000 soldiers is not a joke!' I had often heard people, impressed by their fortitude and resolve, say so.

Besides the disturbing report card of death that the newspapers were, there was another section which brought much solace to me – the obituaries section. I spent most of the time reading those columns without feeling a hint of restlessness. The obituaries were of different kinds: some featured 'Fateh Khwani', or funeral prayers, while some 'Chaharum', or commemoration on the fourth day after the passing, and sometimes, it could even be a simple announcement of a demise – 'Intiqaal Purmalal'. I'd find it consoling to know that people were still dying of old age, illnesses, under ordinary circumstances, of natural causes and some from accidents too. They were fortunate to go without being blown into pieces, dying of stray bullets, or from torture, in massacres, I thought. That section ensured that one didn't have to stare at the grotesque images of mutilated militants or hapless civilians, to be dismissed later as collateral damage. Those faces and scenes remained deeply etched in the memory, sometimes appearing in my dreams, but always sitting in some corner of the mind.

Looking at the faces of the people who had passed on from the world ordinarily made me wish the same for my family and for myself. I wished we'd appear in the section of 'normal' obituaries when our time came, and not hidden in a casualty count on a headline. I'd also do something strange that perversely brought a smile to my face. Most obituaries carried a photograph. I hurriedly signed my name over the tiny portraits of the deceased. To the signature, I added the date and wrote 'Attested' in a running hand. It was something I had picked up from my professor Aunt Nelofar, who was a gazetted officer, and had signed most of my official documents in the same way. Whenever I carried copies of documents that I needed to submit before appearing for my board exams to Aunt Nelofar, I'd be fascinated with how her swift and confident signature deemed them bona fide. I developed a habit of doing the same to obituaries. Somehow, a sense of closure ensued from that act. It was my way of acknowledging the 'normal' deaths and the fact that they were not lumped together, thrown into some unnamed, unmarked grave or a ditch, not denied the dignity of a proper burial. That the deceased would be given the respect that the end of any human life deserves was reassuring; sometimes I'd smile to myself. Bobeh's Chaharum announcement did not carry her portrait, but a sense of ease prevailed inside me to see her name there on the obituaries page.

The potatoes were crackling. They were ready to be eaten. It was time for me to go back home. I folded the newspaper and buried my nose in the yellow turtleneck which I had been wearing the last time I had hugged Bobeh three days ago. It still had a faint smell of her pheran. Or I could at least imagine it to linger. The house I would go back to would be bereft of her presence but filled with her memories. Our home, the little monument of memory.

NOTES

EVENING

The Day I Was Dead

Koche: An alley. The old city of Srinagar is woven and connected by an intricate maze of alleys.

Gul Karfi: 'Gul' is short for Ghulam and 'Karfi' the colloquial term for curfew. Ghulam Mohammad Shah, known as Gul Shah, was the Chief Minister of Jammu and Kashmir from July 1984 to March 1986. He repeatedly imposed curfew in the city during his tenure, which earned him the epithet Gul Curfew or 'Gul Karfi'.

Mushtaq Latram: Mushtaq Ahmad Zargar was the founder of Al-Umar, an active militant outfit of the early 1990s. He was arrested in 1992 and then released in Kandahar in 1999 in exchange of a passenger flight. (There was a running joke about his nickname: Two carpenters, frisked by the troops, were questioned about the contents of their gunny sacks. They replied, 'Keel, Hathoda aur Latram Shatram [Nails, hammer and miscellaneous items]'. The troops then started beating them up, thinking they were teasing them with Latram's name.)

Boher Kadal: Bohri Kadal.

Memory of the Scalp

Seemaab: Quicksilver, mercury. A home remedy used to keep hair free from lice infestations.

Wanwun: An indigenous style of women's singing in chorus, usually at weddings, without the help of any musical instrument.

Taeleem: A rhythmic chant that is hummed by traditional carpet weavers in Kashmir. It is to that mysterious sound flow that they weave carpets.

Maam Toath: A term of endearment for one's maternal uncle, usually used by older generations.

Braandh: The elevated extension of a house, just at the threshold outside the main door.

Yakhyen/Yakhni: A yoghurt based gravy cooked with cinnamon and dried ginger, garnished with dried mint. Cooked in three styles: with mutton, lamb tripe or bitter gourd. At weddings, large meatballs called goshtaab are cooked in this gravy, and it marks the culmination point of a thirty-six course meal.

Zombre Thool: Hard-boiled eggs cooked either with a tomato paste or sliced onions.

Zaene Kadal: Zaina Kadal.

Do Wishes Come True?

Saat-e-Hassan: A supposedly divine moment that has the power of turning anything uttered in that instant true.

Khawaja Khazir: In the Quran, in Surah Al-Qahaf, there is a reference to a mystic who possesses great wisdom. He is found near rivers and streams. His company was sought by prophet Musa, who wanted to witness and understand how the saint receives direct illumination from God. In the Sufi tradition, Khawaja Khazir is believed to have the gift of eternal life.

Kanger: A portable earthen fire-pot. With a wickerwork exterior and a clay interior, it is used to carry hot embers. Essential to surviving bitter cold winters, it is usually carried around under the pheran.

Evening Salute

Waan pyend: The extension of a shop; a spot availed by men in the neighbourhood for passing time. Often used to have witty banter or serious political discussions.

Juloos: Procession.

Nezabaen sunnd tchu bozan Khodah: 'God listens to the voiceless.'

The Metallic Monster

Laalan tchu kormut BA/ BT Haariy kor invarsity saal: A song celebrating the education of newly-weds. It translates as: 'the groom is graduate with a BA/BT, the bride has invited everyone at the university'.

Dass kad nebar tchai qabeel daeri Tcze hav tchi saeri tamahdaar: 'Extend your hand to your guests, all of them are fond of you.'

Hye wayn hez karrini dubareh, diss hez maefi: 'She won't do it again, please forgive her!'

Rituals Old and New

Dum chai: A strong flavoured tea. Made with boiling cinnamon in water for over ten minutes, after which a pinch of green tea is added and the brew is boiled for another minute. Often had post dinner, at the end of a physically exhausting day or to get relief from gastric discomfort.

Malaroat: Malaratta.

NIGHT

When Our Folk Tales Dried Up

Moaj aes jantich hooer: 'Mother was an angel from heaven.'

Tilleh (Tilla): It is one of the most prevalent forms of traditional embroidery in Kashmir. Woven with gold or silver thread on ethnic wear, pherans, or the borders of a shawl, that form a part of every woman's wardrobe. Worn by some elderly ladies as a part of their daily wear, it is included as a part of trousseaus too.

Halam: Lap; the part of a traditional pheran, used to denote the cloth slightly above the hem.

Voal: Waalah. It connotes the male gender of a person.

Heart Goes Boom-Boom

Kafan: A shroud.

Tabaruk/Tobruk: Blessing, benediction. At local shrines in Kashmir, priests keep dates or shireen (sugar balls) in front of them while chanting verses, making the items sacred so that they can be distributed to the devotees. At the Hajj pilgrimage, tabaruk comprises dates, Zam Zam water, skull caps and tasbih (prayer beads).

'*Iss ke liye paisa kahaan se aata hai, saale madarchod aatankvadiyo?*': 'Where does the money for such expensive things come from, you motherfucking terrorists?'

May I Become Invisible, Please?

More than one hardliner factions: Al Baqr, People's League, Wahdat-e-Islam and Allah Tigers had demanded the 'more Islamic' ways of living. After the initial excitement and fear to adhere to the new diktat, the movement gradually lost relevance. After all, the fight wasn't about establishing a religious republic, but about the political aspirations of a people. The struggle has been about their inalienable right to self-determination.

The Country with a Burnt Post Office

Tehreek: In local parlance in Kashmir, it is referred to the beginning of the armed insurgency that erupted against New Delhi in 1989.

Gaw Kadal: On 21 January 1990, hundreds of unarmed protestors defied a civil curfew and shouted slogans of independence. The paramilitary troops of CRPF shot at the crowd. Up to fifty-one civilians were reported to have been killed and hundreds injured. See William Dalrymple, 'Kashmir: The Scarred and the Beautiful', *The New York Review of Books*, 1 May 2008, https://www.nybooks.com/articles/2008/05/01/kashmir-the-scarred-and-the-beautiful/, accessed on 18 January 2021; Also, Victoria Gatenby, 'Kashmiris mark 28th anniversary of Gaw Kadal Mark Anniversary Massacre', Al Jazeera, 21 January 2018, https://www.aljazeera.com/news/2018/01/kashmiris-mark-28th-anniversary-gaw-kadal-massacre-180121185626847.html, accessed on 18 January 2021;

'"Everyone Lives in Fear": Patterns of Impunity in Jammu and Kashmir', Human Rights Watch, 11 September 2006, https://

www.hrw.org/report/2006/09/11/everyone-lives-fear/patterns-impunity-jammu-and-kashmir, accessed on 18 January 2021.

Tengpur/Tengpora: In 1990, mass demonstrations were rampant. Some protestors took out a march to visit the United Nations Military Observer Group in India and Pakistan (UNMOGIP) to submit a memorandum seeking resolution to the Kashmir conflict. In an attempt to stop them, the troops fired on the crowd, killing around twenty-five civilians.

Faheem Aslam, 'Zakura, Tengpora carnages haunt survivors', *Greater Kashmir*, 14 March 2015, https://www.greaterkashmir.com/news/more/news/zakura-tengpora-carnages-haunt-survivors/, accessed on 18 January 2021; and KL News Network, 'March 1, 1990: "The Day When Army Men Fired 47 Dead in Srinagar"', *Kashmir Life*, 28 February 2017, https://kashmirlife.net/march-1-1990-day-army-men-fired-47-dead-srinagar-133692/, accessed on 18 January 2021.

Djinn and Jahanam

Tasruf: To be possessed.

Anti-depressants are colloquially called '*nindreh dawah*' (sleep or calming medication). According to a report released by MSF (Médecins Sans Frontières/Doctors Without Borders) in 2016, 1.8 million Kashmiris (45 per cent of the population) showed symptoms of significant mental distress. See https://www.msfindia.in/msf-scientific-survey-45-kashmiri-population-experiencing-mental-distress/

EARLY HOURS

Pasikdar: The Benign Spirit

Brokus kornam kaanyen raatas: 'The spirit kept crushing my sides all night.'

Ayat-al-Kursi: Called the 'Verse of the Throne', it is a specific verse from the Quran which is known to protect its reciter. Our parents and grandmother would encourage us to say it before going to bed in order order to avoid nightmares and to stay safe from evil spirits and jinns.

The Door on the Floor

Apne gharoon se baahar nikaliyey. Koi aadmi ghar pe na paaya jaaye: 'Come outside of your houses. No man should be found inside his house.'

Crackdown: An impromptu siege would be announced on loudspeakers from the mosques or whizzing jeeps in a neighbourhood. It'd start at any part of the day. Back in the 1990s, it'd mostly begin soon after morning prayers and last from a few hours to a couple of days. All the houses would be thoroughly searched and ransacked during this time. The male members of the family were assembled in large grounds or compounds of local schools, sometimes in sub-zero temperatures, and the women and children remained petrified at home. The men were queued up and paraded in front of a gypsy that had a police informer, commonly known as Mukhbir, sitting inside, who'd identify militants or militant suspects. Crackdown is now termed as CASO (cordon and search operation). See '"Everyone Lives in Fear"'.

I Miss Walking

Girde, lawase, baker-khani: Various types of bread eaten at different hours of the day. While preparing girde (also called czot) in the tandoor, the pattern of the baker's fingertips forms on top of the bread. Lawase is an unleavened bread and had with morning tea. It is also used as a wrap for roadside barbecued meat (tujje). Baker-khani is a wafer-like bread which is served to guests or had during the four o'clock teatime instead or along with tczochvoar.

Kyenz: A copper bowl with an elevated hollow base. The base has an intricate pattern carved on it that differentiates it from a Toor or a Bushkaab which have ornate solid bases.

DAWN

Forbidden Courtyard

Poand: The then currency denomination in the form of a brass coin.

Kreth: The stinging and burning sensation caused from the smoke created during tempering, especially when spices are added to hot, boiling oil.

Asr: The third of the five obligatory daily prayers in Islam.

Trath Peynakh: 'May lightning fall upon them.' 'Trath', meaning lightning, is usually used as a curse, but can also be used to describe a stunning woman. *'Trath hish'* translates into 'lightning-like'.

Surah Fheel: Faith in the Faith

Wapas pheyr sa hye, ati tchuui jang chalaan!: 'Turn around, there is a war going on there!'

Shadow of a Siege

Tokke kor: An ethnic gold bangle with two open ends. Each end has a snakehead design. Some snakeheads are embellished with tiny, glittering semi-precious stones fitted in the place of their eyes.

Lal Chowk fire: After a gun-battle in Lal Chowk, troops had set ablaze an entire patch of shops. In April 1993, *The New York Times* reported that Indian security forces had been blamed for arson and killings across Srinagar. See, Asia Watch, A Division of Human Rights Watch and Physicians for Human Rights, 'Violations by Government Forces', in 'The Human Rights Crisis in Kashmir: A Pattern of Impunity', p. 57, https://www.hrw.org/sites/default/files/reports/INDIA937.PDF; also Nisar Dharma, 'April 10, 1993: The day a boat sank with the dead', FreePress Kashmir, 10 April 2018, https://freepresskashmir.news/2018/04/10/april-10-1993-day-boat-sank-with-the-dead/, accessed on 18 January 2021.

Moi-e-Muqadas: A strand of hair of Prophet Mohammad (PBUH).

Vejbyoar/Bijbehara: Protests erupted in the valley against the siege laid on the Hazratbal shrine. In one such protest in Vejbyoar, the troops (74th Battalion of Border Security Force), in an attempt to disallow the crowd from moving forward, fired on it killing up to fifty civilians. See '"Everyone Lives in Fear"'; also Majid Maqbool, 'At Bijbehara, Site of 1993 Massacre, the Killing of 43 Kashmiris is Still a Raw Wound', The Wire, 22 October 2017, https://thewire.in/rights/twenty-four-years-after-kashmirs-bijbehara-massacre-victims-still-wait-for-justice, accessed on 18 January 2021.

Cinemas? No Scope!

Lion of the Desert that had instigated anti-Sheikh Abdullah sloganeering and protests in the 1980s: The dialogue from the 1981 war film *Lion of the Desert*, 'We will not surrender. We win or we die', uttered by the film's protagonist Omar Mukhtar, a Libyan tribal leader, gained extreme popularity in Srinagar when it was released and inspired a whole generation. The lines continue to be quoted in the current times.

A Wedding, a Funeral

Traem/Trami: A medium-sized copper plate on which food is served during weddings and shared amongst four people. It comes with a concave lid called sarpoash.

Muss miczraven: A pre-wedding ceremony held before the bride's henna ceremony. The bride is surrounded by her relatives and friends who have to undo the multiple plaits that are braided by her friends. As they proceed with the activity, trinkets such as combs, hair clips, hair pins and ribbons are distributed among young girls.

MORNING

Speech Impediments

Taavan ha pyoam: 'A curse has fallen upon me.'

Hedwun: Headwin, pronounced as 'Hedwun', is the informal name for the SMHS hospital near Government Medical College, Srinagar. It was named after an Austrian trader and philanthropist, Headow, who donated his estate for the construction of the first state hospital.

Curfew as Poison

Wurusi: Certain architectures allow carved wooden planks to form partitions in a room. Usually three in number, these planks are adjustable and can be stacked up together inside an arched, hollow cove to allow more space between two chambers. Or else, these are brought down and act as a wooden wall between the chambers or rooms.

Goshtaab: A big meatball. It is cooked with Yakhyen/Yakhni, a yoghurt-based gravy made with dried ginger, cinnamon, and dried and crushed mint leaves. That dish marks the culmination of a feast at a wedding or a celebration.

Power blackout: Black Day was observed on specific dates which included 27 October (Accession Day), 26 January (India's Republic Day) and 15 August (India's Independence Day). It culminated in a power blackout when all lights were switched off in the evening. To avoid even the slightest flicker escaping out, we covered small windowpanes, without curtains, with a blanket or some dark coloured cloth.

Memory of the Lake

Sanam sunte hain teri bhi kamar hai/Kahaan hai, kis taraf hai, kidhar hai?: 'Beloved, they say you possess a waist/Where is it? Which side, where indeed?'

The couplet by Urfi, a sixteenth-century Persian poet, can be translated into: 'Such is the climate of Kashmir/it will regrow the feathers of a burnt bird.'

The other couplet referred to is by Amir Khusro.

Gar Firdaus Ba Roye'n Zameen Ast/Hamee(n) asto. Hamee(n) asto. Hamee(n) asto. It can be translated as: 'If there is a paradise on earth/it is here, it is here, it is here.'

Aya ba daanish gah rafta boodi?: 'Had you gone to the university?'

Rafta boodam, rafta boodam!: 'Yes, I had, yes, I had.'

The local UN office: Refers to the office of the United Nations Military Observer Group in India and Pakistan (UNMOGIP).

Shared Grief

Zanneh nyoov jenazeh malaikav vidaan vidaan: 'As if the angels flew his coffin away.'

CRP: Informally used for Central Reserve Paramilitary Forces (CRPF).

'A hereditary Islamic leader, the most senior and influential opponent of Indian rule in Kashmir, was assassinated in his home in the state's capital today. When 100,000 angry mourners followed his body through the streets of the city, security forces opened fire, killing at least 30 people and wounding some 200, according to hospital doctors.' (Barbara Crossette, 'Muslim Leader of Kashmir Slain; 30 Die as Police Fire on Mourners', Special to the *New York Times,* https://www.nytimes.com/1990/05/22/world/muslim-leader-of-kashmir-slain-30-die-as-police-fire-on-mourners.html, accessed on 18 January 2021.)

See also, Faisul Yaseen, '25 Years of Deceit: Hawal Massacre Inquiry Yet to Take Off, *Rising Kashmir,* 21 May 2015, http://www.risingkashmir.in/news/25-years-of-deceit-hawal-massacre-inquiry-yet-to-take-off, accessed on 18 January 2021; Arif Shafi Wani, 'Hawal massacre anniversary: "It Was Hell; Saw Paramilitary Men Firing with Machine Guns on Civilians"', *Greater Kashmir*, 21 May 2015, https://www.greaterkashmir.com/news/kashmir/hawal-massacre-anniversary-it-was-hell-saw-paramilitary-men-firing-with-machine-guns-on-civilians/, accessed on 18 January 2021.

Naareh: Slogans.

Jis Kashmir ko khoon se seencha, Woh Kashmir humara hai: 'The Kashmir that has been irrigated with our blood, that Kashmir belongs to us.'

Of Men, Mice and Violence

Khyeczir: A porridge made of rice and lentils, flavoured with salt and cumin.

Jajeer: A traditional hookah with a copper or brass base.

AFTERLIFE

Q.K.: The Courtyard Graffiti

Livun: A light variant of water-based chalk paint that came in two colours – white and green. A coat or two of this was applied to the walls to keep them from looking weather-beaten.

Khoda karih sahlei: 'Allah will have mercy.'

The Saintless

Aastaan: A shrine.

Tobruk/Tabaruk: Benediction or a blessing.

Resh sund Tobruk: Benediction received at the shrine of the Sufi master Baba Payyam udin Reshi. The shrine is situated near Tangmarg en route to Gulmarg.

Tczochvoar: A bagel-shaped bread with sesame seeds sprinkled on it. It is had with the 4 o'clock salty tea, nun chai.

Etiqaad: Belief.

Sounds and the Silencer

Zuv hai vandai: A term of endearment which literally means 'my life for yours'.

Games Our Children Play

Pre-Tehreek: The decades before 1989.

Mushir-ul-Haq: Mushir-ul-Haq was a non-Kashmiri vice chancellor of Kashmir University in 1990. He was kidnapped on 6 April 1990, along with his personal secretary Abdul Gani Zargar. The militant outfit that had abducted them were demanding the release of militants from prisons. When the state didn't comply, the duo was killed and their bodies were found on 10 April 1990.

The Dread of Dastarkhwaan

Dastarkhwaan: Tablecloth.

Aloo-bukhara chicken: A chicken dish cooked with dried plums that impart a tangy taste to the curry.

Tczaek waangan: Aubergines cooked with tamarind pulp.

Namda: An embroidered light rug made by felting sheep fleece.

ACKNOWLEDGEMENTS

Firstly, I must thank Ananth Padmanabhan for believing in this book when all I had was just the title.

For its title, I thank Agha Shahid Ali and his poetry that has been a place of refuge for years.

Mirza Waheed, for his sincere friendship.

Sohini Basak, my editor, for shaping this book and bringing a sense of stillness to my thinking.

Udayan Mitra, Publisher – Literary at HarperCollins India, for his reassuring comments.

In Delhi, Gurgaon, Mumbai: Arunav Gogoi, Sfoorti Sachdeva, and Amrita Goswami and her table.

In Washington D.C.: Agnès Bun, for creating our own maps of travel and a dictionary of typos.

In Singapore: Ketna Patel, Jayapriya Vasudevan, Nomita Dhar, Raju Gopalakrishnan and Pamposh Dhar, for opening their hearts and homes to me.

My Kashmiri friends: Ruwa Shah, Fozia and Sidiq, Inshah Malik, Cuhail, Sadaf and Sumi.

In Kerala: Thommen Jose, for his kindness.

My colleagues: Anand Murthy, Subbu, Shriram Iyer, Rajiv Chatterjee, Rana Barua and Vishnu Mohan, for their support.

Professor Iffat Maqbool, for her erudition and being of utmost help towards the completion of the final draft.

Rafiq Kathwari, for his exacting feedback on the first draft of the book.

Amandeep Sandhu, for his forthrightness.

Dr Nagpal, for his empathetic association over the years.

The song '*Roz Roz*' by Parvaaz that held me together after the 5 August 2019 lockdown.

The by-lanes of downtown Srinagar, the shrine of Shah Hamdan, which keep me equanimous.

Dr Nisar Mir, for his support and love during some of the darkest times. Thank you, Uncle Nisar.

My parents: Bashir, for teaching us the value of travel and exploration; Rashida, for being the ever-giving spring of Persian literature. Thank you both for your unique layers of love.

Bushera Bashir, for never leaving my side no matter what.

Matthys Boshoff, for reinforcing my faith in humanity and love.

Roshina, for her resilience.

Lastly, I thank Father, Mother and Bobeh (Ghulam Hassan Ghani, Atiqa Hassan, Sarwa Begum) – the three members of my family who rest in the graveyard next to the shrine of Khankah-i-Maula but continue to live on in my heart.

ABOUT THE AUTHOR

Farah Bashir was born and raised in Kashmir. She was a photojournalist with Reuters and currently works as a communications consultant. *Rumours of Spring* is her first book.